HOW TO FIND YOURSELF AFTER HEARTBREAK

A JOURNEY TO OWN SELF - 7 STEP GUIDE

DEEPA SAINI

To My Dearest Mother & Father,

From my very first step to the dreams, I chase today, your unwavering love and belief in me have been my greatest strength. You stood beside me through every challenge, lifting me up when I stumbled and cheering the loudest in my moments of triumph.

Your sacrifices, your endless patience, and the quiet strength with which you shaped my journey are the foundation of everything I am today. This book is not just my work—it is a reflection of your trust in me, a testament to the values you instilled, and a tribute to the unconditional love that has been my guiding light.

With all my heart, I thank you. This is for you.

Contents

Foreword

"Healing is not about getting over it; it's about getting through it, step by painful step, until you find yourself again."

Preface

INTRODUCTION

Heartbreak isn't just about romantic love – it can be from friendships, career failures, or betrayal.

Heartbreak isn't just about lost love; it may also be caused by broken friendships, work setbacks, or unanticipated betrayals. It's the pain of lost trust, the sting of unrealized goals, and the void left by those who walked away. Pain takes many forms, but so do healing, resilience, and the will to move on.

And I strongly believe that, there is no one who has not experienced it in their lifetime, doesn't matter how hard we try to avoid it.

Heartbreak is way more painful than just an emotional wound—it affects our mind, body, and spirit. It doesn't matter whether it is caused by a romantic breakup, the loss of a friend, betrayal, or a life-changing event, heartbreak always leaves us with the of feeling lost and disconnected from our true selves.

But very few knows that within this pain lies an opportunity of knowing & understanding our real YOU !

CHAPTER ONE

UNDERSTANDING HEARTBREAK AND ITS IMPACT

"Don't cry when the sun is gone, because the tears won't let you see the stars."

— VIOLETA PARRA

A broken heart is not merely a figure of speech; it represents a genuine psychological experience that can leave profound and enduring marks on our mental state. The anguish of heartbreak is a shared human experience, one that crosses cultural and generational boundaries, affecting countless individuals throughout history. Despite its widespread nature, the significant effects of lost love on our emotional and mental health are often overlooked.

At its core, heartbreak embodies the intense emotional suffering and turmoil that arises when a romantic relationship ends or when love is unreturned. It encompasses a complex mix of feelings, including sadness, anger, confusion, and despair. While we typically link heartbreak to the conclusion of romantic partnerships, it's essential to recognize that similar emotions can emerge from other types of loss, such as the heart-wrenching experience of losing a child.

The frequency of heartbreak in our society is astonishing. Research from the American Psychological Association indicates that more than 85% of adults have faced at least one significant romantic heartbreak in their lives. That's a staggering number of shattered hearts! Understanding the psychological ramifications of this common yet deeply personal experience is vital for several reasons.

Firstly, heartbreak is not just a brief moment of sorrow; its effects can invade our psyche, shaping our thoughts, actions, and even our physical health. By exploring the psychological consequences of heartbreak, we can better prepare ourselves and others to navigate the challenging emotional landscape that follows.

The Immediate Impact: When Love Leaves The Building

Imagine this scenario: you're enjoying your day, feeling great, when suddenly – BAM! – your partner drops the "we need to talk" bombshell. In an instant, your world is turned upside down. This is the immediate aftermath of heartbreak. The first and most apparent response is emotional pain, and it can be excruciating.

Many people describe this feeling as a physical ache, highlighting just how deeply heartbreak can affect us.

What Leads To Heartbreak?

We've all experienced that gut-wrenching moment when someone we care about causes us pain, leaving us engulfed in disappointment and heartache. The emotional turmoil can be overwhelming, as a single event can drastically shift our mood and perspective. So, what really triggers heartbreak? Why does it hurt so deeply? Let's delve into the psychology behind this painful experience.

One significant factor contributing to heartbreak is unmet expectations.

In romantic relationships, these expectations can often be unrealistic. Whether it's unreciprocated feelings, a relationship that didn't pan out, or feelings of betrayal, we may find ourselves holding onto hopes that don't align with reality. When those hopes are dashed, it can lead to profound emotional distress, making us feel as though something precious has been lost.

This sense of loss can leave us feeling exposed and vulnerable. To safeguard our emotions, we often establish boundaries in our relationships; when those boundaries are crossed, it can evoke feelings of betrayal, abandonment, and an overwhelming mix of sorrow and anger.

It's essential to recognize that every relationship is unique, even if they share common elements. Always be attentive to the signs that indicate whether your boundaries are respected. If they aren't, take a moment to reflect on the situation to better understand it, which will help you navigate future relationships with greater awareness. This proactive approach can empower you to manage your emotions and avoid unnecessary pain that may lead to further heartbreak.

Heartbreak is more than just an emotional experience

It's a profound physiological event that reshapes the way we perceive ourselves and the world. When we lose someone or something meaningful, our brain processes it similarly to physical pain. Studies have shown that heartbreak activates the same neural pathways as physical injury, which is why it feels so overwhelming and consuming.

Why Pain Feels So Intense?

Our brain creates emotional connections and stories.

One of the famous FMRI study (read: study using a brain scanner showing film activity in the brain) shows that the same part of the brain activated by physical pain is activated due to emotional pain after separation.

This does not mean you will necessarily experience the same type of pain as an injury. But this means that even a small rejection is aware of the potential threat to your survival.

The same level of threat as physical damage. It shows that our brains have developed to focus our attention on threats and focus our attention on them (don't look away or be distracted) and we believe it protects us. It is due to what is considered dangerous.

It's no wonder that it makes us feel so bad. They are not just emotionally processed. They are interpreted as threats to our survival. This means that our brains are focused on them and fixed on them, treating them as damage.

The emotional and physical effects of heartbreak can be intense. It can lead to anxiety, depression, insomnia, loss of appetite, and even a weakened immune system. Our minds become trapped in repetitive thought patterns, replaying memories, searching for closure, or internalizing blame. This emotional turmoil doesn't just affect our mood—it alters our self-identity, making us question our worth, choices, and ability to move forward.

Sometimes, it even goes beyond our irritable mood and can even turn into the dark thoughts of self-harm & in rare cases could even go to suicide thoughts.

I have experienced myself that even the carrier setback – which might not sound like even comparable to romantic heartbreak can lead to anxiety & depression & makes you feel all broken. It impacts our mental health and which in turn - negatively affects out physical health....and life seems so difficult and not worth living.

But beyond the pain, heartbreak disrupts our sense of self, which is very dangerous thing. This disrupted sense of self makes each day a turmoil. Relationships, friendships, or careers all these shape our identity, and when they end abruptly, we feel lost. The familiar future we envisioned disappears, leaving behind uncertainty.

This shift can be disorienting, but it also presents a unique opportunity—to rebuild ourselves with greater awareness and strength.

"Heartbreak is a setback—but it could be an opportunity to transform, rediscover our authentic selves, and take charge of our emotional well- being. "

CHAPTER TWO

STEP 1 : ACCEPT & ACKNOWLEDGE YOUR PAIN

"Healing begins the moment you accept that something hurt you."
— YUNG PUEBLO

The importance of facing emotions instead of suppressing them. We inhabit a world where many of us feel uneasy about our emotions. Society often conditions us to view these feelings as obstacles rather than valuable insights.

Navigating our emotions can be daunting and overwhelming, particularly if we haven't learned how to do so or if we haven't had support during tough emotional times. It's something we all face at various points in our lives. Many people resort to suppressing their emotions as a way to cope with challenging, intense, or unwelcome feelings.

If you find yourself doing this frequently, it doesn't mean there's something wrong with you; it simply has its limitations in certain situations. This response is quite natural, especially when there is a lack of trust or safety within your family or social environment, making it hard to be vulnerable and express your feelings. While this emotional defense mechanism aims to shield us, relying on it too much can drain essential mental and physical energy that could be better spent on important daily activities like work, studying, spending time with family, or engaging socially.

In a society that often promotes constant movement and positivity, it can be easy to overlook or dismiss uncomfortable feelings. Emotions like sadness, anger, and frustration may feel like unwelcome intruders, prompting many of us to steer clear of them. However, what if the path to improved well-being lies in fully embracing these negative emotions? By allowing ourselves to experience our feelings deeply, we can unlock significant benefits that foster emotional, mental, and spiritual growth.

For some reason, it is seen in our society as a weakness in how we feel. Because of this, most people suppress how they feel every day, which can lead to a rather multiple problems. Society appears to praise that feeling to hide, but this means that they retain all the problems that deviate, rather than letting them free and find a solution.

You have to take the time to feel the emotions, rather than filling them up. It's much better to release your emotions than to allow them to mess with and intensify. When expressing your feelings to yourself, give them the opportunity to find solutions to problems and emotions.

Instead of running away, they appear in the minds of emotions.

I see you now, old silent friend,
The ache I tried so hard to bend.
You sat in corners of my chest,
Unspoken truths I once suppressed.
I wore a smile, a clever guise,
While sorrow hid behind my eyes.
But pain, you never sought to flee—
You waited there to set me free.
You taught me strength is not the fight,
But letting darkness meet the light.
Not pushing tears behind a door,

But letting sorrow wash the shore.
You held a mirror to my soul,
Revealing wounds that made me whole.
Not broken, no—but deeply real,
With scars that know, and scars that heal.
So here I stand, no more afraid,
No need for mask, no need to fade.
I speak your name, I feel your flame,
And in that fire, I reclaim my name.
For pain is part of being true—
A quiet bridge from me to you.
And every tear that once I shamed
Now blooms with strength I've softly claimed.

Accepting Emotions Transform Lives

Emotional Release and Relief

When we permit negative emotions to emerge, we create an opportunity for release. Ignoring feelings such as sadness or anger can lead to a buildup of internal pressure, which may manifest as anxiety, stress, or even physical ailments. While it might seem easier to bottle up these emotions, doing so often comes with consequences. In contrast, acknowledging and feeling these emotions allows them to flow through us, providing relief and helping to prevent emotional congestion over time.

Think of it like a river; when it flows freely, everything is in harmony, but when it gets blocked, pressure accumulates until it bursts forth. Our emotions function similarly. By allowing them to flow naturally, we can avoid the buildup of tension and more easily return to a state of tranquility.

Self-Awareness and Growth

Welcoming all emotions, particularly the challenging ones, enhances our self-awareness. It gives us the opportunity to examine what triggers specific feelings and why they resonate so strongly within us. This heightened awareness serves as a valuable tool for introspection and personal development. By gaining insight into our emotional reactions, we can uncover underlying needs or unfulfilled desires, enabling us to address them in a constructive manner.

For example, feelings of frustration may indicate a need for change or highlight a boundary that has been crossed. By recognizing these emotional cues, we can make necessary adjustments in our lives, leading to a healthier and more balanced mindset.

Building Resilience

Engaging with negative emotions can also foster resilience. It's important to understand that processing these feelings equips us with the strength to navigate future challenges.

Understanding how to manage your emotions without pushing them down is essential. When faced with challenging feelings, people typically respond in one of two ways: they either express their emotions outwardly or bottle them up. Acting out, especially with intense emotions like anger, can lead to negative repercussions in your relationships, work, and leisure activities.

This outward expression often generates a cycle of anger that complicates matters further. On the other hand, suppressing these strong emotions can be even more harmful in the long run.

What many may not realize is that there is a healthier approach to emotional regulation: **experiencing your feelings as they arise.**

Emotions can be likened to energy waves, fluctuating in form and intensity, much like the waves of the ocean. They naturally come and go, and when we try to interfere with this process—whether by acting out or suppressing —we can encounter various issues. Ironically, trying to "talk yourself out of" your emotions often leads to increased rumination, causing you to dwell on the very feelings you wish to escape. Those who have experienced a deep-tissue massage can attest to how the body retains suppressed emotions. This suppression can manifest physically and lead to a range of problems, including anxiety, depression, stress-related illnesses, and even more severe outcomes like substance abuse and suicidal thoughts.

There are strong reasons why you should express yourself rather than filling your feelings.

Here are 10 reasons you should never suppress your emotions:

"Unexpressed emotions will never die. They are buried alive and will come forth later in uglier ways."

– Sigmund Freud

You may forget more. Stanford University research shows that their random memories are influenced by emotional repression, as long as they are buried.

They often process memories at night while they dream. Therefore, if you suppress your feelings, you will realize that you have fewer dreams.

Dreams help you solve things in your daily life. Of course, most people don't want to remember what they think causes them pain, and this idea of ignoring the memory or emotion helps them overcome the incident.

However, this can lead to more problems on the street as emotions inevitably come to the surface. You will feel mentally tired & overwhelmed because of the energy needed to remind you of a smile, while you feel the world is falling apart around them. This is normal. Because it seems that everyone who tries to maintain quietness while dealing with negative reactions seems to be drained.

The key is not to prevent your emotions from coming to you, **give them the outlet.**

As we say, flowing water is always fresh – the moment we try to store it, it starts losing it sheen. Same is true for storing emotions and not let them flow. If you have a healthy outlet for music, drawing, writing, training, etc., you can release your feelings and maintain a balanced mindset.

Your sleep will be impacted negatively

If you hold your feelings down, wake up at night and think about the problems you are facing.The longer you deny problems and emotions in your daily life, the more you deal with insomnia.

Research shows that insomnia can cause mood problems, especially when most nights of the week occur.Of course, a low mood can lead to insomnia throwing and spinning.Either way, you should tackle your repressed emotions so that you can sleep well at night.

Your physical health can be reduced

The same Stanford research confirmed that suppressed emotions, causing memory problems where hidden negative emotions can lead to cardiovascular problems.

When cortisol levels rise and suppress emotions, your heart rate, blood pressure, and breathing increase.To prevent the reaction from impairing physical health, you should exercise at least 30 minutes a day and maintain a healthy diet.

You can gain weight by suppressing your emotions

Many people who have negative answers to them find an outlet for comfortable food.

They experience better and offer temporary relief, but unfortunately can cause a variety of health issues.

Foods for emotional suppression can cause problems such as hypertension, cardiovascular disease, obesity, and diabetes. Foods keep you in your feelings, just creates an unhealthy cycle of emotion of feeling sick, dealing with emotions and gaining weight.

If you use food to deal with emotions, consult a therapist or other licensed professional who can help you. And make sure that this condition is not left untreated.

Your digestion can be painful

From annoyed stomachs and ulcers to acidic reflux and constipation, suppressing emotions can lead to many different digestive problems. Stress of adherence to negative emotions can send your body into combat modes or combat modes, which can ruin your internal systems.

You can see that stress can change bacteria in the intestine, causing it to expand or feel like a gas.

The temporal lobe, a part of the brain near the forehead, can help you finish it off and throw it away with negative emotions if it doesn't help you survive.

Unfortunately, this part of the brain is affected when you hold back your feelings.

Understanding Acceptance

Acceptance is not about giving up or resigning oneself to misery. Instead, it is about acknowledging reality without judgment. It means facing pain, loss, or hardship with an open heart and a willingness to experience emotions fully. Acceptance allows us to shift from a mindset of resistance to one of understanding, leading to inner peace and clarity.

Many people struggle with acceptance because they fear that acknowledging pain will make it more real or unbearable. However, the opposite is true—when we accept our emotions and experiences, we release the emotional resistance that makes suffering worse. This allows us to move through pain rather than getting stuck in it.

How Acceptance Paves The May For Healing

Reduces Emotional Suffering

Resisting painful emotions often intensifies them. For example, when we suppress grief, it manifests in anxiety, anger, or depression. By accepting emotions as they arise, we allow ourselves to process them naturally, reducing their grip over us.

Fosters Self-Compassion

Many people blame themselves for their struggles, believing they should have acted differently. Acceptance fosters self-compassion, helping us recognize that we are human and that experiencing pain is a natural part of life. This gentle approach allows for greater emotional resilience and self- love.

Encourages Letting Go

Holding on to past hurts, regrets, or anger only deepens emotional wounds. Acceptance enables us to release the need to change the past and instead focus on healing in the present. Letting go does not mean forgetting but rather releasing the emotional charge that keeps us stuck.

Acceptance and Physical Healing

Research has shown that acceptance also plays a critical role in physical healing. Stress and resistance can exacerbate health conditions, while a state of acceptance reduces anxiety, lowers cortisol levels, and promotes overall well-being. Studies suggest that individuals who accept their illnesses— rather than fighting or denying them—tend to have better health outcomes and improved quality of life.For example, individuals with chronic pain who practice acceptance experience less suffering than those who constantly resist their condition.

By acknowledging pain without letting it define them, they find ways to live fulfilling lives despite their limitations.

Cultivate Acceptance

Acknowledge Your Feelings

Instead of ignoring or suppressing emotions, allow yourself to feel them fully. Journaling, meditation, or speaking with a trusted friend can help you process emotions healthily.

Practice Mindfulness

Mindfulness helps ground us in the present moment, preventing us from getting lost in past regrets or future anxieties. When we focus on the now, we cultivate a sense of peace and acceptance.

Reframe Negative Thoughts

Instead of seeing challenges as unfair, try to view them as opportunities for growth. Ask yourself, "What can I learn from this? How can this make me stronger?"

Seek Support

Healing does not have to be a solitary journey. Seeking help from a therapist, support group, or close friends can provide guidance and comfort along the way.

"Acceptance is the foundation of healing."

By opening up and accepting reality, we release unnecessary suffering and create space for growth, peace and transformation.

Whether it is emotional wounds, physical complaints, or healing from previous trauma, acceptance allows us to move forward with strength and grace. The earlier you accept it, the more you can enter what you can.

CHAPTER THREE

STEP 2 : LETTING YOURSELF MOURN

"Give yourself permission to feel it all. The pain, the emptiness, the silence. Mourning is how your heart tells the truth to your soul."
- Deepa Saini

Heartbreak, no matter how it happens, leaves behind echoes of what once was. Letting go is not about forgetting but about freeing yourself from the chains of the past. It's about making peace with what happened and moving forward with strength. In this chapter, we explore practical ways to let go, with real-life stories from India that inspire hope and healing.

How To Stop Replaying Memories

One of the hardest parts of moving on is breaking the loop of memories that keep playing in our minds. Whether it's a song, a place, or a message that brings back old feelings, these memories can trap us in the past. Overcoming this requires a conscious effort to change our focus and redirect our emotions toward the present and future.

Our minds have a tendency to replay painful or nostalgic memories, keeping us trapped in the past. Whether it's a moment of regret, loss, or a time when things felt better, these repetitive thoughts can be emotionally exhausting. Overanalyzing the past prevents us from fully engaging in the present and moving forward. Breaking free from this cycle requires conscious effort and practical strategies.

In this chapter, we will explore why we replay memories, the impact it has on our well-being, and how to shift our focus to the present.

Why Do You Replay Memories?

Replaying memories is a natural function of the brain. It can be a way of learning from past experiences, finding closure, or even seeking comfort. However, when these memories become intrusive or obsessive, they can hinder personal growth. Some common reasons for replaying memories include:

- **Unresolved Emotions** – When we haven't fully processed an event, our minds keep returning to it in an attempt to make sense of it.
- **Regret and Guilt** – Wishing we had acted differently or made better choices can lead to endless mental loops.
- **Nostalgia and Longing** – Missing a past relationship, job, or time in life can make the present feel unfulfilling.
- **Fear of the Future** – Sometimes, we replay past situations to predict or control what might happen next.Understanding why we revisit certain memories is the first step in learning to manage them effectively. There are real negative Impact of replaying memories. While reflecting on the past can be useful in moderation, excessive rumination can be harmful. Constantly reliving past events can lead to:
- **Increased Anxiety and Depression** – Dwelling on negative experiences fuels stress and emotional pain.
- **Disconnection from the Present** – Focusing too much on what was prevents us from appreciating what is happening now.
- **Lowered Self-Esteem** – Replaying failures or mistakes reinforces feelings of inadequacy and self-doubt.

- **Difficulty Moving On** – Staying stuck in the past prevents personal growth and new opportunities.

To break free from this cycle, we need to actively redirect our thoughts and develop new coping mechanisms.

Acknowledge and Accept

The first step is to recognize when you are stuck in a cycle of replaying memories. Instead of fighting it, acknowledge the thought and accept that it is part of your experience. This allows you to distance yourself from the emotional charge of the memory.

Shift Your Focus to the Present

Engage in mindfulness practices such as deep breathing, meditation, or grounding exercises. Bringing attention to your senses—what you see, hear, and feel—helps disrupt repetitive thought patterns.

Challenge the Memory

Ask yourself: "Is this memory serving me?" If it's a regret, what lessons can you take from it? If it's nostalgia, what aspects of the present can you appreciate? Reframing your thoughts can reduce their emotional hold over you.

Limit Triggers

Identify and minimize situations that bring back unwanted memories. This could include social media, certain songs, or places that remind you of the past.

Redirect Your Energy

Replace rumination with positive actions. Exercise, hobbies, journaling, or spending time with loved ones can shift your focus away from the past.

Seek Closure

If a memory lingers due to unresolved emotions, find ways to create closure. This could be writing a letter (even if you never send it), having a conversation, or practicing forgiveness—either for yourself or someone else.

Practice Self-Compassion

Be kind to yourself. Everyone has regrets and painful memories. Remind yourself that you did the best you could with the knowledge and resources you had at the time.

Replaying memories can keep us stuck in a loop of emotional distress, but we have the power to break free. By understanding why we dwell on the past, recognizing its impact, and implementing practical strategies, we can reclaim our mental space. Focusing on the present, finding closure, and practicing self-compassion are key steps toward letting go and embracing the future. Life is happening now—don't let yesterday's memories hold you back from today's happiness.

Battle Mith Nostalgia

Aditi, a software engineer from Bangalore, found herself stuck in an endless cycle of painful memories after her five-year relationship ended. She would revisit old WhatsApp conversations, scroll through photos, and replay their favorite songs. Each time, she felt the same heartbreak all over again, preventing her from moving forward.

Aditi decided to take control. She started journaling her feelings daily, noting every time she felt the urge to revisit the past. This helped her recognize how these habits were deepening her sadness. Gradually, she began replacing old triggers with new experiences. She redecorated her apartment, changed her music playlist, and planned weekend trips with friends. Over time, she noticed a shift—while the past still existed, it no longer controlled her present.

Solution: Identify your triggers and replace them with new experiences. Create fresh memories—travel to a new place, listen to different music, or redecorate your space to signal a fresh start. Engaging in mindfulness techniques like meditation and grounding exercises can also help center your thoughts in the present moment.

Understanding Unhealthy Attachments

In today's digital world, moving on is harder because social media keeps us connected to people even when they are no longer in our lives. Seeing their updates, photos, or even indirect mentions can reignite old emotions, making it difficult to heal. While the idea of unfollowing, muting, or blocking someone might feel drastic, it is often necessary for emotional well-being.

Unhealthy attachments can hold us back, whether they stem from toxic relationships, past traumas, or self-destructive habits. These attachments keep us emotionally entangled, making it difficult to move forward and embrace a healthier, more fulfilling life. Letting go is not easy, but it is necessary for growth and well-being. In this chapter, we will explore the nature of unhealthy attachments, their impact, and effective strategies to break free.

An unhealthy attachment is any emotional bond that causes more harm than good. It may stem from fear, insecurity, or a need for validation. Some common types of unhealthy attachments include:

- **Toxic Relationships** – Staying in relationships that drain energy, cause emotional pain, or prevent personal growth.
- **Past Traumas** – Holding onto painful memories or unresolved emotions that dictate present behavior.
- **Unrealistic Expectations** – Clinging to an idealized version of a person, relationship, or life event that may never exist.
- **Codependency** – Relying too heavily on another person for happiness and self-worth.
- **Addictions and Bad Habits** – Forming emotional reliance on substances, behaviors, or unhealthy coping mechanisms.

Understanding these attachments is the first step toward breaking free.

Impact of holding on to harmful attachments can have a profound effect on mental, emotional, and even physical well-being. Some common consequences include:

- **Emotional Exhaustion** – Constantly investing in toxic people or unhealthy habits drains emotional energy.
- **Lack of Personal Growth** – Staying stuck in the past prevents progress and new opportunities.
- **Low Self-Morth** – Depending on external factors for validation diminishes self-confidence and independence.
- **Increased Anxiety and Stress** – Fear of letting go can create ongoing emotional turmoil.

Recognizing these effects can motivate us to take action and release what no longer serves us. To cut off unhealthy attachments, try these points, and see how effective these strategies are :

Acknowledge the Attachment

The first step is awareness. Identify what or whom you are attached to and recognize why it is unhealthy. Acceptance of the situation makes it easier to initiate change.

Set Boundaries

Establish firm boundaries with people or situations that drain you. This may mean reducing contact, saying no, or distancing yourself from harmful influences.

Practice Self-Reflection

Ask yourself, "Why am I holding on to this? What do I fear will happen if I let go?" Understanding the root cause of the attachment can help you address it.

Replace with Positive Habits

When breaking free from an unhealthy attachment, fill the void with positive activities such as exercise, hobbies, or meaningful relationships.

Seek Support

Whether through friends, family, or professional therapy, having a support system can make the process of detachment easier and provide emotional guidance.

Let Go of Guilt and Fear

Many attachments persist due to guilt or fear of the unknown. Remind yourself that prioritizing your well-being is not selfish; it is necessary for growth.

Practice Self-Love

Focus on self-care, affirmations, and activities that boost confidence. The stronger your self-worth, the less likely you are to cling to toxic connections.

Cutting off unhealthy attachments is a powerful act of self-liberation. By identifying toxic connections, setting boundaries, and prioritizing self-care, we create space for healing and personal growth. Letting go is not about forgetting but about freeing yourself from what holds you back. Embrace the process, trust yourself, and make room for healthier, more fulfilling relationships and experiences in your life.

Social Media Detox

Rohan, a college student from Delhi, had a difficult breakup but struggled to move on because his ex-girlfriend's updates kept appearing on his feed. Seeing her happy without him made him question his self-worth. He constantly compared his progress to hers, deepening his emotional distress.

A friend advised him to take a social media detox. At first, Rohan resisted, fearing he would miss out on important updates. However, he eventually deactivated his Instagram for a month, choosing to focus on fitness and a new hobby—photography. During this time, he rediscovered personal joy and built new routines that were not influenced by his past relationship.

When he returned to social media, he no longer felt the urge to check his ex's profile.

Solution: If seeing someone's updates affects your peace, take a break from social media. Unfollow accounts that trigger old emotions, mute or block if necessary, and engage in activities that uplift you. Filling your life with positive engagements will naturally reduce your dependence on past attachments.

Understanding Guilt, Regret, And Self-Blame

Many people hold onto the past because they feel responsible for how things ended. They wonder if they could have done something differently, replaying scenarios in their minds. But self-blame only keeps you stuck in an endless cycle of guilt, preventing growth and self-acceptance.

Guilt, regret, and self-blame are powerful emotions that can weigh us down, keeping us stuck in the past and preventing personal growth. While it's natural to reflect on past mistakes or missed opportunities, dwelling on them excessively can lead to emotional distress and hinder our ability to move forward. Overcoming these feelings requires self-compassion, perspective, and proactive steps toward healing. In this chapter, we will explore the causes of guilt, regret, and self-blame, their impact, and strategies to release them.

Guilt arises when we feel responsible for a wrongdoing, whether real or perceived. Regret stems from wishing we had made different choices, while self-blame often involves harshly criticizing ourselves for past actions. These emotions can result from:

- **Past Mistakes** – Actions we believe hurt ourselves or others.
- **Unrealistic Expectations** – Holding ourselves to impossible standards.
- **Cultural or Societal Pressure** – Feeling guilty due to imposed norms or values.
- **Survivor's Guilt** – Experiencing guilt for thriving when others have suffered.

Recognizing these causes is essential to moving toward resolution and self- forgiveness.

Impact Of Holding On To Emotions

Unresolved guilt, regret, and self-blame can have profound emotional and psychological effects, including:

- **Low Self-Morth** – Constantly blaming ourselves erodes confidence and self-esteem.
- **Increased Anxiety and Depression** – Ruminating on the past can lead to emotional distress.
- **Fear of Moving Forward** – Guilt can make us hesitant to take new risks or embrace happiness.
- **Strained Relationships** – Holding onto guilt can make it difficult to connect with others in a healthy way.

By recognizing these effects, we can take steps to free ourselves from these burdens. There are few strategies, implementing which we can overcome the burden of guilt, regret & self balme.

Acknowledge Your Emotions

The first step to healing is acknowledging how you feel without suppressing it. Accept that guilt, regret, and self-blame are natural human emotions.

Differentiate Between Healthy and Unhealthy Guilt

Healthy guilt leads to growth and change, while unhealthy guilt keeps us stuck. If your guilt helps you learn and improve, use it constructively. If it only causes suffering, it's time to let it go.

Practice Self-Compassion

Remind yourself that you are human and that mistakes are part of life. Treat yourself with the same kindness and understanding you would offer a friend.

Make Amends Where Possible

If your guilt is tied to past actions, consider apologizing or making amends. However, if this is not possible, focus on learning from the experience and moving forward.

Reframe the Situation

Instead of seeing past mistakes as failures, view them as lessons that helped shape you. Ask yourself, "What did I learn from this experience?"

Challenge Negative Self-Talk and replace self-criticism with affirmations and reminders that you are worthy of forgiveness and happiness. Engage in Mindfulness and Gratitude. Ground yourself in the present through mindfulness practices. Gratitude helps shift your focus from what went wrong to what is going right.

Seeking Support is sometime necessary and we should never shy away from doing that just because of society taboo. Talking to a therapist, support group, or trusted loved ones can provide perspective and help you process emotions in a healthy way.

"Overcoming guilt, regret, and self-blame is essential for emotional well-being. "

By practicing self-compassion, making amends when possible, and reframing negative thoughts, we can release these burdens and move forward with peace. Healing does not mean forgetting the past—it means learning from it and allowing ourselves the freedom to grow.

Journey To Self-Forgiveness

Self-forgiveness is an essential yet often challenging part of healing. When we hold onto guilt, regret, or self-blame, we create barriers that prevent us from fully embracing our growth and happiness. True forgiveness does not mean excusing mistakes but rather accepting them, learning from them, and allowing ourselves to move forward without carrying the weight of past actions. This chapter explores the importance of self-forgiveness, the challenges it presents, and the steps we can take to achieve it.

Importance Of Self-Forgiveness

Forgiving ourselves is crucial for emotional well-being and personal growth. It allows us to:

- **Heal from Emotional Mounds** – Letting go of past mistakes helps us move forward with a lighter heart.
- **Build Self-Compassion** – Accepting our imperfections fosters a healthier relationship with ourselves.
- **Reduce Anxiety and Stress** – Self-forgiveness minimizes the burden of guilt and allows for inner peace.
- **Enhance Relationships** – When we forgive ourselves, we become more open and compassionate toward others.

Why Is Self-Forgiveness Difficult?

Many people struggle with self-forgiveness due to deep-seated guilt, fear of repeating past mistakes, or the belief that they must punish themselves.

Common barriers include:

- **Perfectionism** – Holding ourselves to unrealistic standards makes it difficult to accept mistakes.
- **Fear of Accountability** – Some believe forgiving themselves means avoiding responsibility.
- **Societal or Cultural Conditioning** – Messages from society, religion, or upbringing may reinforce guilt and self- blame.
- **Emotional Attachments** – Staying connected to guilt can feel like honoring a past event or person.
- Recognizing these barriers is the first step toward overcoming them.

Steps To Self-Forgiveness

- **Acknowledge the Mistake** : Self-forgiveness starts with recognizing what happened without denial or avoidance. Accept responsibility without allowing it to define you.

- **Understand the Impact** : Reflect on how your actions affected yourself and others. This step promotes awareness and personal growth.
- **Separate Your Actions from Your Identity** : A mistake does not define your entire character. You are more than your past choices.
- **Practice Self-Compassion** : Treat yourself with the kindness you would extend to a close friend. Everyone makes mistakes—what matters is how we learn from them.
- **Make Amends Where Possible** : If your actions affected others, an apology or an effort to repair the situation can help both you and them move forward.
- **Reframe Your Perspective** : Instead of dwelling on regret, focus on the lessons learned. Ask yourself, "How has this experience helped me grow?"
- **Release the Need for Punishment** : Forgiveness is about healing, not self-inflicted suffering. Remind yourself that you deserve peace and happiness.
- **Embrace the Present and Future** : Shift your focus from the past to what you can do today to create a better future.

The journey to self-forgiveness is a transformative process that requires self-awareness, compassion, and a willingness to grow. By acknowledging our mistakes, making amends, and embracing the lessons they offer, we free ourselves from the burden of guilt and self-blame. Forgiving yourself is not a sign of weakness—it is a testament to your strength and commitment to living a fulfilled, authentic life.

Meera, a 38-year-old teacher from Chennai, blamed herself for her divorce. She kept thinking, "If only I had been more patient, things could have worked out." This self-blame drained her emotionally and kept her stuck in a painful loop. She withdrew from friends and hesitated to pursue happiness, believing she didn't deserve it.

One day, she attended a healing retreat where she participated in a self- forgiveness exercise. The instructor asked her to write a letter to herself, expressing everything she felt without judgment. As she wrote, she realized that she had done her best with the knowledge and resources she had at the time. She slowly started shifting her mindset, acknowledging that blaming herself was preventing her from healing.

Solution: Write a letter to yourself or the person you parted ways with (you don't have to send it). Express everything you feel and forgive yourself for any mistakes. Accept that every experience, even painful ones, contributes to personal growth. Therapy, self-help books, or talking to a trusted friend can also provide guidance in overcoming guilt.

The Power Of Forgiveness (For Yourself And Others)

Forgiveness doesn't mean you have to accept what happened as right. It simply means you refuse to carry resentment in your heart. When you forgive, you free yourself from the pain of the past, allowing new joy and peace to enter your life. Holding onto anger or resentment only prolongs your suffering.

Forgiveness is a profound and transformative act that has the power to heal wounds, strengthen relationships, and bring inner peace. Whether directed toward ourselves or others, forgiveness is not about condoning hurtful actions but about releasing resentment and pain.

Holding onto grudges, guilt, or anger only prolongs suffering, whereas forgiveness liberates us to embrace a future free from the burdens of the past. This chapter explores the importance of forgiveness, the challenges it presents, and the steps to cultivate it in our lives.

Forgiveness benefits both the forgiver and the forgiven. It allows us to:

1. **Heal Emotional Wounds** – Letting go of resentment and guilt alleviates emotional pain and promotes healing.
2. **Break Free from the Past** – Forgiveness frees us from the weight of past mistakes and grievances, allowing for personal growth.
3. **Reduce Stress and Anxiety** – Carrying anger or guilt increases emotional distress; forgiveness fosters inner peace.
4. **Strengthen Relationships** – Forgiveness helps rebuild trust and understanding in relationships that have been strained by hurt.
5. **Improve Overall Well-Being** – Studies show that people who practice forgiveness experience lower blood pressure, improved mental health, and a greater sense of happiness.

Why Is Forgiveness Difficult?

Many struggle with forgiveness because of deep emotional wounds, fear of vulnerability, or the belief that forgiving means forgetting or excusing harmful behavior. Common barriers include:

Holding onto Anger – Feeling justified in our resentment can make forgiveness seem unnecessary.

Fear of Being Hurt Again – Forgiving can feel like making ourselves vulnerable to further pain.

Lack of Closure – When we don't receive an apology or acknowledgment of wrongdoing, it can be harder to let go.

Self-Punishment – Some believe they don't deserve forgiveness and continue punishing themselves for past mistakes.

Recognizing these barriers is essential to overcoming them and embracing the power of forgiveness.

Forgiving yourself can be very difficult, and believe it's even harder than forgiving others. But we can start this journey by **acknowledging our mistakes.** Accept responsibility without allowing past actions to define you.

Understand the Impact, reflect on how your choices affected yourself and others. Separate your actions from your identity. You are more than your past choices; they do not define your worth.

Practice self-compassion, Treat yourself with kindness and understanding.

Make Amends Where Possible and If you hurt others, apologize sincerely and seek to repair the damage. Reframe the Situation - Focus on what you have learned rather than dwelling on regret. **Let go of the guilt** - recognize that you deserve to move forward with peace.

And once you are comfortable in your own skin, start forgiving others by :

Acknowledge Your Pain : Recognize the hurt and allow yourself to feel it fully.

Empathize with the Other Person : Try to understand their perspective without justifying their actions.

Release the Need for Revenge : Letting go of anger does not mean letting go of justice, but it frees you from bitterness.

Decide to Forgive : Forgiveness is a choice, not a feeling—commit to the process even if it takes time.

Communicate If Possible : If it feels safe and necessary, express your forgiveness to the other person.

Focus on the Present and Future : Don't let past pain dictate your happiness; focus on what lies ahead.

The power of forgiveness lies in its ability to set us free—from guilt, anger, and emotional burdens. Forgiving yourself and others is not about excusing harmful actions but about choosing to prioritize your own peace and growth. By embracing forgiveness, we create space for healing, stronger relationships, and a future filled with love and understanding. Let go, move forward, and reclaim your joy.

Path To Letting Go

Arjun, a businessman from Mumbai, was betrayed by his best friend, who also happened to be his business partner. The betrayal cost him money and emotional trust. For years, Arjun carried the bitterness with him. Every time he saw someone succeed in business, he felt his own wounds reopen.

One day, a mentor advised him, "Holding onto anger is like drinking poison and expecting the other person to suffer." This struck a chord with Arjun.

He realized that while his former friend had moved on, he was still living in resentment. Slowly, Arjun shifted his focus from bitterness to rebuilding his business. He invested in new projects, formed meaningful relationships with ethical partners, and found success. Over time, he realized that letting go of anger gave him the energy to move forward.

Solution: Understand that forgiveness is for you, not for the other person. Holding onto anger only harms you. Meditation, therapy, or even a simple self-reflection exercise can help you let go. Write down what you learned from the experience and how it has made you stronger. Practicing gratitude for the lessons learned can also aid in releasing resentment.

Letting go of the past is a journey, not a one-time decision. It takes courage to release painful memories, break unhealthy attachments, overcome self- blame, and practice forgiveness. Every small step you take brings you closer to a lighter heart and a brighter future. Like Aditi, Rohan, Meera, and Arjun, you too can find your way forward. The past is a place of reference, not residence. It's time to turn the page and start a new chapter of your life.

Emotional healing is a path that many individuals take after experiencing trauma, loss, or significant internal challenges. Central to this journey is a concept that may seem straightforward yet is often quite intricate: acceptance.

We frequently hear that emotional healing requires us to "accept" our experiences or feelings. But what does acceptance truly entail in this context? More importantly, how can something that appears passive, like acceptance, facilitate deep and active healing?

This is where the paradox emerges.

Acceptance in the realm of emotional healing is frequently misinterpreted. Many of us equate it with giving in or resigning ourselves to unchangeable circumstances.

It can feel like a passive act, suggesting that accepting our pain means we are okay with our suffering or powerless to change our situation. In reality, acceptance is anything but passive; it is an active and dynamic process that paves the way for healing by allowing us to let go of resistance instead of succumbing to defeat.

To unravel this paradox, we must first clarify **what acceptance truly means?**

It is not about agreeing with or justifying what has happened to us. Instead, acceptance involves recognizing the reality of our circumstances, our emotions, and our wounds without judgment or denial.

It requires us to understand that our feelings—whether they are pain, sadness, or anger—are valid and arise for a reason. Often, we instinctively want to push these emotions away because they are uncomfortable or even overwhelming. However, when we deny or suppress these feelings, they tend to linger and grow stronger, much like trying to keep a beach ball submerged in water.

Genuine acceptance enables us to conserve our energy by no longer resisting our emotions, allowing us to begin the journey of understanding and working through them. Recognizing feelings of inadequacy is the first step toward healing.

Acceptance involves understanding that these emotions are present for a reason. Once we acknowledge their existence, we can start to delve into their origins and gradually work on healing ourselves.

The intriguing aspect of acceptance is that it can lead to transformation by allowing things to remain unchanged for a while. When we embrace our emotions or past experiences, we create an environment where these feelings can flow through us instead of becoming stagnant. This process is essential for initiating healing.

It's common for individuals to struggle with codependency, where they may feel an overwhelming need for validation from others. This desire can trap them in a cycle of pleasing others, leading to frustration when they can't break free. However, by accepting their codependent tendencies and understanding that these behaviors often stem from past coping mechanisms, they may find that the pressure to change diminishes. This acceptance creates an opportunity to explore the roots of these patterns and gently begin to shift away from them.

"Healing often arises not from forcing change but from embracing our current state and allowing it to evolve "

STEP 3 : REBUILDING SELF- WORTH

"You alone are enough. You have nothing to prove to anybody."
— *MAYA ANGELOU*

Heartbreak doesn't just break your heart—it often shatters your confidence, self-image, and sense of worth. Whether it's a relationship, a betrayal, or a loss, the emotional pain can leave you questioning your value. However, self-worth is not dependent on anyone else. It is an internal belief, one that you can rebuild stronger than before. This chapter explores practical ways to regain confidence, establish self-respect, and embrace a renewed sense of self.

Understanding Self-Worth

Self-worth is the foundation of how you view yourself. It is not based on your relationship status, job, or achievements—it comes from within. When heartbreak shakes your confidence, it's crucial to remember that your value is inherent, not dependent on external validation.

Self-worth is the foundation of our confidence, emotional resilience, and overall well-being. It shapes the way we perceive ourselves, how we interact with others, and the decisions we make in life. Understanding self- worth is not about external validation or achievements but recognizing our intrinsic value as individuals. This chapter explores the meaning of self- worth, its importance, common challenges in developing it, and practical steps to cultivate a strong sense of self-worth.

When we have a strong sense of self-worth, we are better equipped to handle life's challenges, build healthy relationships, and pursue our goals with confidence. The benefits of self-worth include:

Emotional Resilience – A strong sense of self-worth helps us navigate setbacks and challenges without feeling defeated.

Healthy Relationships – When we value ourselves, we set boundaries and surround ourselves with people who respect us.

Inner Peace – Self-worth allows us to find contentment within ourselves rather than seeking approval from others.

Confidence and Growth – Believing in our worth encourages us to take risks, embrace new opportunities, and pursue personal growth.

Once we start understanding the importance of self -worth to cultivate self- worth, then comes the step by step process of building the self-worth :

- **Acknowledge Your Inherent Value** - Your worth is not defined by accomplishments, status, or validation from others—it is intrinsic.
- **Challenge Negative Thoughts** - Replace self-doubt with affirmations and positive self-talk.
- **Set Boundaries** - Prioritize your well-being by saying no to situations or people that diminish your self-worth.
- **Surround Yourself with Supportive People** - Engage with people who uplift and encourage you rather than those who bring negativity into your life.

- **Celebrate Your Strengths and Achievements** - Acknowledge your progress, no matter how small, and take pride in your unique qualities.
- **Practice Self-Compassion** - Treat yourself with kindness and understanding, especially in moments of struggle.
- **Engage in Activities That Bring You Joy** - Pursue hobbies, interests, and goals that reinforce your sense of fulfillment and purpose.
- **Focus on Personal Growth** - Self-worth grows when we invest in learning, growth, and self-improvement.

Understanding and cultivating self-worth is a lifelong journey, but it is one of the most valuable investments we can make in ourselves. When we recognize our intrinsic value, we empower ourselves to lead fulfilling lives, build meaningful relationships, and navigate challenges with confidence.

By embracing self-worth, we step into our power and create a life rooted in self-respect, self-love, and authenticity.

Journey To Self-Worth

Nisha, a fashion designer from Mumbai, found herself struggling after her fiancé broke off their engagement. For months, she believed she wasn't 'good enough'—not pretty enough, not successful enough. Her self-esteem plummeted, and she withdrew from social events.

One day, a mentor told her, "Your worth isn't measured by someone's inability to see it." This struck a chord. Nisha started therapy, practiced self- affirmations, and engaged in her passion for design. She created a new clothing line inspired by resilience, proving to herself that her value wasn't tied to anyone's opinion.

Solution: Recognize that your worth is intrinsic. Engage in self-reflection exercises, such as writing down your strengths and achievements. Therapy or talking to a trusted mentor can help reinforce this mindset.

Overcoming Negative Self-Talk

After a breakup, it's common to fall into patterns of self-criticism—thinking you weren't enough or that you made too many mistakes. But self-worth grows when you replace negative self-talk with positive affirmations.

Negative self-talk can be one of the biggest barriers to personal growth, confidence, and happiness. The way we speak to ourselves internally influences our beliefs, emotions, and actions. When we engage in self- criticism, doubt, or harsh judgment, we limit our potential and reinforce feelings of unworthiness. Overcoming negative self-talk requires awareness, intentional effort, and self-compassion. This chapter explores the impact of negative self-talk, why we fall into this pattern, and practical strategies to shift towards a more positive and empowering inner dialogue.

Persistent negative self-talk can have profound consequences on mental and emotional well-being. Some of the common effects include:

Lowered Self-Esteem – Constantly criticizing yourself diminishes confidence and self-worth.

Increased Anxiety and Stress – Negative thoughts fuel worry and fear, creating a cycle of stress.

Self-Sabotage – Doubting your abilities can prevent you from taking opportunities or pursuing goals.

Strained Relationships – Negative self-perception can make it difficult to connect with others authentically.

Depression and Hopelessness – Persistent self-criticism can lead to feelings of sadness and helplessness.

Overcome Negative Self-Talk

- **Recognizing Your Inner Critic** - Awareness is the first step. Pay attention to your thoughts and identify negative patterns.

- **Challenge and Reframe Negative Thoughts** - Ask yourself: "Is this thought really true?" Replace self- criticism with constructive and encouraging statements.
- **Practice Self-Compassion** - Treat yourself with the same kindness and understanding you would offer a friend.
- **Use Positive Affirmations** - Replace negative thoughts with affirmations that reinforce self-worth, such as "I am capable" or "I deserve happiness."
- **Surround Yourself with Positivity** - Engage with people who uplift and encourage you rather than those who reinforce negativity.
- **Limit Exposure to Triggers** - Reduce time spent on social media or other influences that fuel comparison and self-doubt.
- **Engage in Activities That Boost Confidence** - Pursue hobbies, learning experiences, or achievements that reinforce your strengths and abilities.

Overcoming negative self-talk is a continuous process that requires practice and patience. By becoming aware of destructive thought patterns and replacing them with self-compassion and positivity, you can break free from the cycle of self-doubt. When you speak to yourself with kindness and encouragement, you create a mindset that empowers you to embrace challenges, build confidence, and live with greater self-acceptance and joy.

Battle Against Self-Doubt

Arjun, a software engineer from Bangalore, constantly blamed himself for his failed marriage. Every time he made a mistake at work, he'd tell himself, "I can't do anything right." This self-talk eroded his confidence and affected his performance.

Arjun decided to change the narrative. Every time he had a negative thought, he countered it with evidence of his strengths. He also kept a gratitude journal, listing three things he did well each day. Over time, his mindset shifted, and so did his confidence.

Solution: Challenge your negative thoughts by asking, "Would I say this to a friend?" And if the response is negative, it clearly means you are very harsh on yourself. Replace self-criticism with self-compassion. Daily affirmations and gratitude journaling can help rewire your thought patterns.

Setting Boundaries And Prioritizing Self-Respect

When you rebuild self-worth, setting boundaries becomes essential. Boundaries protect your energy, time, and emotions from people or situations that drain you.

Boundaries for a Fresh Start

Priya, a marketing professional in Delhi, always put others first. After a toxic relationship, she realized she had let people walk over her emotions. She decided to set firm boundaries—saying 'no' when necessary, limiting contact with toxic individuals, and prioritizing self-care. Though it was difficult at first, she found that people who respected her boundaries also valued her more.

Solution: Learn to say 'no' without guilt. Identify areas in your life where you feel drained and set clear boundaries. Surround yourself with people who uplift and respect you.

Rediscovering Passions And Hobbies

Rebuilding self-worth means reconnecting with activities that bring you joy. Hobbies and passions provide a sense of accomplishment, reminding you of your unique talents and interests.

ife's demands often push personal interests and hobbies to the background. However, engaging in activities that bring joy and fulfillment is essential for overall well-being. Rediscovering passions and hobbies is a powerful way to reconnect with yourself, boost creativity, and enhance emotional health. This chapter explores the importance of hobbies, reasons we lose touch with them, and practical steps to reignite passion for what truly makes us happy.

The Importance of Engaging in Hobbies

Incorporating hobbies into daily life has numerous benefits, including:

1. **Improved Mental Health** – Engaging in activities you love reduces stress, anxiety, and depression.
2. **Enhanced Creativity and Problem-Solving** – Hobbies stimulate the mind and encourage innovative thinking.
3. **Increased Self-Confidence** – Mastering a new skill or revisiting a passion builds self-esteem and personal growth.
4. **Emotional Fulfillment** – Doing what you love fosters a sense of joy, purpose, and contentment.
5. **Stronger Social Connections** – Many hobbies offer opportunities to meet like-minded individuals and build supportive communities.

Why We Lose Touch With Our Passions

Many factors contribute to losing interest in hobbies and passions, such as:

Busy Schedules and Responsibilities – Work, family, and daily obligations can take precedence over personal interests.

Self-Doubt and Fear of Failure – Feeling inadequate or comparing oneself to others can discourage participation.

Lack of Motivation – Over time, interests may fade due to exhaustion or burnout.

Life Transitions – Major changes such as moving, career shifts, or personal loss can shift focus away from hobbies.

Cultural or Societal Expectations – External pressures may lead individuals to prioritize productivity over personal enjoyment.

But when heartbreak happens, unfortunately we have all the time in the world, as we don't feel like doing anything, and most of time we are sitting and stuck in the loops of overthinking. So, once we understand - what we were before hearbreak and accept with undertstanding the reasons behind, it's time to rediscover your passions and hobbies :

Reflect on Past Interests

Think about activities you once enjoyed but stopped doing. What made them fulfilling?

Try New Experiences

Exploring unfamiliar hobbies can spark excitement and reveal hidden talents.

Make Time for Yourself

Set aside dedicated time for hobbies without feeling guilty about it.

Remove Perfectionism and Pressure

Engage in hobbies for enjoyment rather than achievement or external validation.

Reconnect with Like-Minded People

Join clubs, groups, or online communities that share similar interests.

Incorporate Hobbies into Your Routine

Integrate your passions into daily or weekly schedules to make them a habit.

Celebrate Small Wins

Acknowledge progress and effort rather than focusing on mastery or end results.

Allow for Evolution

Interests may change over time. Be open to exploring new passions without limitations. Rediscovering passions and hobbies is a journey of self-exploration and joy. By making space for personal interests, you create a more balanced, fulfilling life that nurtures creativity and emotional well-being. Hobbies are not just pastimes; they are powerful tools for self-expression, growth, and inner peace. Embrace what excites you, and allow yourself to thrive in the pursuit of passion.

The Power Of Positive Influences

The people you spend time with influence your self-worth. Being supportive, uplifting individuals helps reinforce a positive self-image.

The people we surround ourselves with have a significant impact on our mindset, self-esteem, and overall well-being. Positive influences uplift, inspire, and support us, while negative influences can drain energy and hinder personal growth. Being intentional about who you allow into your life is a key step in fostering a healthier and more fulfilling existence. This chapter explores the importance of positive relationships, how to identify beneficial influences, and steps to create an uplifting social environment.

Choosing the right people to surround yourself with brings numerous benefits, including:

1. **Enhanced Self-Confidence** – Supportive relationships reinforce self-worth and help you believe in your abilities.
2. **Increased Motivation and Growth** – Encouraging influences push you to strive for personal and professional success.
3. **Emotional Mell-Being** – Positive people contribute to a more joyful, stress-free life.
4. **Healthier Mindset** – Being around optimistic individuals fosters a positive outlook on challenges and setbacks.
5. **Greater Accountability** – Friends and mentors who genuinely care about you help keep you on track with your goals.

Identifying Positive And Negative Influences

Recognizing who adds value to your life and who depletes your energy is essential. Consider these distinctions:

Positive Influences: Supportive, uplifting, encouraging, honest, kind, and growth-oriented individuals.

Negative Influences: Judgmental, discouraging, manipulative, overly critical, or emotionally draining people.

Ask yourself:

Do I feel energized or drained after spending time with this person?

Do they inspire and encourage my growth, or do they hold me back?

Are they genuinely happy for my success, or do they react with jealousy and negativity?

Surround Yourself With Positive Influences

1. **Evaluate Your Current Relationships** : Reflect on who adds value to your life and who may be holding you back.
2. **Seek Out Like-Minded Individuals** : Engage in communities, social groups, or professional networks that align with your values and aspirations.
3. **Limit Exposure to Negative Influences** : Distance yourself from toxic relationships that no longer serve your well-being.
4. **Set Healthy Boundaries** : Protect your energy by clearly defining what behaviors you will and won't tolerate.
5. **Be the Positive Influence You Seek** : Cultivate kindness, encouragement, and authenticity in your own interactions.
6. **Find Mentors and Role Models** : Surround yourself with people who inspire and challenge you to grow.
7. **Engage in Positive Environments** :Participate in uplifting activities such as personal development workshops, hobby groups, or volunteering.

Surrounding yourself with positive influences is a conscious choice that leads to personal fulfillment and growth. The right people will lift you up, encourage your ambitions, and help you navigate life's challenges with resilience. By carefully curating your social environment, you cultivate a life filled with encouragement, inspiration, and emotional well-being.

Choose wisely, and embrace the power of positive connections.

Support System

Karan, a student from Pune, felt lost after his girlfriend left him. He isolated himself, which deepened his loneliness. A childhood friend noticed his withdrawal and encouraged him to join a fitness group. Through the new friendships he formed, Karan regained a sense of belonging and motivation.

Solution: Identify who uplifts you and spend more time with them. If needed, seek support groups or professional guidance. Being around positivity helps you believe in yourself again.

Rebuilding self-worth is not an overnight process—it's a journey of rediscovering your inner strength, setting boundaries, engaging in passions, and surrounding yourself with positive influences. Just like Nisha, Arjun, Priya, Rohit, and Karan, you have the power to redefine your worth. You are enough, just as you are.

CHAPTER FIVE

STEP 4 : REDISCOVERING WHO YOU ARE

"You were never really lost. You were just buried under someone else's expectations."

— Norman Vincent Peale

Heartbreak often leaves people feeling lost, as if a part of their identity was tied to the relationship that ended. But this phase also presents a unique opportunity—to rediscover who you are

beyond relationships, redefine your happiness, and explore aspects of yourself that may have been overlooked. This chapter guides you through the journey of self-exploration, helping you reconnect with your passions, dreams, and authentic self.

Identifying What Makes You Happy Beyond Relationships

When in a relationship, it's common to intertwine happiness with the presence of another person. After a breakup, it becomes essential to rediscover independent sources of joy. True happiness comes from within and is shaped by your interests, values, and aspirations.

Journey To Personal Joy

Heartbreak can be an overwhelming experience, but it also presents an opportunity to rediscover joy and fulfillment within yourself. Personal joy is not dependent on another person—it comes from within, built on self- awareness, gratitude, and purpose. This journey requires healing, self-love, and a commitment to embracing life with a renewed sense of happiness and fulfillment.

Nidhi, a software engineer from Mumbai, realized after her breakup that most of her social activities revolved around her partner's preferences. She struggled with loneliness until she began experimenting with different hobbies—reading fiction, learning photography, and joining a trekking group. Through this process, she discovered that solitude wasn't lonely; it was an opportunity to connect with herself.

Solution: Make a list of activities that once made you happy before the relationship. Try new things that spark curiosity. Find joy in small moments, such as watching the sunset, listening to music, or cooking for yourself.

Your journey to personal joy is about reclaiming your happiness and recognizing that fulfillment comes from within. By embracing self-love, gratitude, and new opportunities, you create a life that is rich, meaningful, and full of joy. Heartbreak is just a chapter—not the whole story. The best part of your journey is yet to come.

Exploring Hobbies, Passions, And New Experiences

Hobbies are not just leisure activities; they are powerful tools for healing and self-expression. Trying new things allows you to step outside your comfort zone and build confidence.

Heartbreak can leave you feeling lost, as if a piece of your identity has been taken away. However, this period of healing is also an opportunity for self- discovery. By exploring new hobbies, passions, and experiences, you can reconnect with yourself, find new sources of joy, and build a fulfilling life beyond your past relationship.

Why Hobbies And Passions Matter In Healing

Engaging in activities you enjoy serves as a form of therapy, helping to shift your focus from pain to personal growth. Here's how hobbies can aid in healing:

Distraction from Emotional Pain – Immersing yourself in something new helps break the cycle of rumination.

Boosting Self-Esteem – Mastering a skill or learning something new fosters confidence and self-worth.

Creating Positive Associations – Engaging in fulfilling activities replaces old, painful memories with joyful new ones.

Building New Social Connections – Joining hobby-based communities introduces you to like-minded individuals who support your growth.

Rediscovering Old Passions

Sometimes, heartbreak makes us realize how much we've neglected personal interests. Take time to revisit activities that once brought you happiness.

- **Did you used to love painting, writing, or playing music?** Pick up your brush, pen, or instrument again.
- **Were you passionate about fitness or outdoor adventures?** Reignite your love for hiking, running, or yoga.
- **Did you enjoy cooking or baking?** Experiment with new recipes and flavors to nourish both body and soul.

Reconnecting with past passions can help reestablish a sense of familiarity and comfort in your life.

Discovering New Interests

Heartbreak presents an opportunity to step outside your comfort zone and reinvent yourself. Trying new activities allows you to explore uncharted aspects of your personality and interests.

Creative And Artistic Outlets

Expressing emotions through creativity is therapeutic. Consider:

- Painting, Sketching, or Pottery – Artistic activities provide a visual and emotional outlet.
- Photography – Capturing the beauty around you shifts focus from internal sadness to external inspiration.
- Creative Writing or Journaling– Writing your thoughts down can be a powerful form of self-reflection and healing.

Physical Activities For Mental And Emotional Strength

Exercise releases endorphins, improving mood and reducing stress. Try:

- Yoga and Meditation – Helps in calming the mind and improving emotional regulation.
- Dance Classes – Freely expressing yourself through movement can be liberating.
- Martial Arts or Strength Training – Builds resilience, both physically and mentally.

Adventure And Travel

New experiences help break old patterns and provide fresh perspectives. Explore:

- Solo Travel – Discovering new places alone boosts confidence and self-sufficiency.
- Road Trips with Friends – Strengthens bonds and creates positive memories.
- Outdoor Adventures – Activities like hiking, kayaking, or camping reconnect you with nature.

Social And Learning-Based Activities

Expanding your knowledge and social circle can help with healing. Try:

- Taking a Class or Workshop – Learning a new language, coding, or playing an instrument keeps your mind engaged.
- Joining a Book Club – Reading and discussing books with others promotes intellectual and emotional growth.
- Volunteering – Helping others fosters a sense of purpose and fulfillment.

How To Get Started

1. **Make a List of Interests** – Write down activities you've always wanted to try or hobbies you previously enjoyed.
2. **Start Small** – Begin with one or two new activities to avoid feeling overwhelmed.
3. **Join a Community** – Whether online or in-person, connecting with others makes hobbies more enjoyable.
4. **Give Yourself Time** – Healing and rediscovering joy is a gradual process. Be patient with yourself.
5. **Celebrate Progress** – Acknowledge small victories, whether it's mastering a new skill or simply enjoying a new experience.

Heartbreak no doubt is painful, but it also provides an opportunity for renewal. Exploring hobbies, passions, and new experiences helps you heal by giving you purpose, joy, and confidence. By embracing this period of self-discovery, you open doors to a life filled with happiness, growth, and meaningful experiences.

Self-Reflection Activities (Who Was I Before? Who Do I Want to Be Now?)

Understanding your personal evolution is key to moving forward. Self- reflection allows you to assess past experiences, learn from them, and define your future goals.

Path To Self-Discovery

Heartbreak can feel like losing a part of yourself, leaving you questioning your identity and purpose. However, this painful period can also be an opportunity for deep self-discovery. When a relationship ends, you have a chance to reconnect with who you truly are, independent of anyone else.

Embracing this journey with openness and curiosity allows you to rebuild a fulfilling and meaningful life.

"In the quiet after shattered dreams,
A whisper stirs beneath the seams.
Not broken—just a page unturned,
A softer flame that still has burned.
You search the cracks, the silent space,
And slowly meet your own true face.
No longer lost in someone's light,
You find your voice, your inner might.
The world looks new through tear-washed eyes,
With dawns that rise from old goodbyes.
Heartbreak may bruise, but it won't bind—
For love begins when you you find. "

Self-Discovery After Heartbreak

Allow Yourself To Feel

Healing starts with acknowledging and accepting your emotions. Suppressing pain can delay growth, while embracing it allows you to move forward. Journaling, therapy, or speaking with a trusted friend can help process your feelings in a healthy way. Spiritual practices like meditation, prayer, or mindfulness can also provide inner peace and clarity, helping you trust the journey of healing.

Reflect On Your Relationship

Use this time to analyze what you learned from your past relationship:

- What did the relationship teach you about love, trust, and compatibility?
- Were there patterns in the relationship that didn't serve you well?
- What qualities do you want in future relationships?

From a spiritual perspective, *view the relationship as a chapter in your soul's evolution*. Every experience, including pain, serves a purpose in your growth. Trust that the universe or a higher power is guiding you toward something better aligned with your true self.

Reconnect With Your Passions

Many people lose themselves in relationships, putting personal interests aside. Now is the time to reconnect with activities that bring you joy.

Whether it's painting, music, reading, or fitness, pursuing what excites you can be a powerful way to reclaim your identity. Engaging in creative or meditative activities, such as writing, painting, or yoga, can also connect you with your higher self, allowing you to heal on a deeper level.

Explore New Experiences

Trying new things can be a great way to discover hidden talents and interests. Consider:

- Traveling to a new place
- Learning a new skill or language
- Taking up a creative or physical hobby

Spiritually, new experiences can help you embrace the idea of flow— trusting that life is unfolding as it should. Letting go of control and surrendering to new adventures can lead to unexpected joy and transformation.

Cultivate Self-Love And Self-Morth

True self-discovery comes from recognizing your value outside of a relationship. Practice self-care by:

- Speaking kindly to yourself
- Prioritizing mental and physical well-being
- Setting healthy boundaries in all relationships

Spirituality can play a crucial role in self-love. Practices like gratitude, affirmations, and connecting with nature can help you feel supported by a greater force, reminding you that you are inherently valuable and loved.

Heartbreak can be painful, but it also serves as a doorway to self-discovery. By reflecting, exploring new passions, and embracing your individuality, you can emerge from this experience stronger, wiser, and more aligned with your true self. Viewing this journey through a spiritual lens allows you to see heartbreak as a stepping stone to personal and spiritual awakening.

Trust that this experience is leading you to something greater—a life filled with love, peace, and purpose.

Meera, a fashion designer from Bangalore, journaled about her past self— her dreams before the relationship, the values she had compromised, and the lessons she learned. This exercise helped her recognize her strengths and redefine what she wanted in life.

Solution: Try self-reflection exercises:

- **Journaling:** Write about your past aspirations and current desires.
- **Meditation:** Spend quiet time reflecting on your emotions.
- **Vision Boards:** Create a collage of your future goals and dreams.

By rediscovering who you are, embracing your passions, and reflecting on your journey, you gain the power to shape a fulfilling and independent life after heartbreak.

STEP 5 : STRENGTHENING MINDSET

"Change your thoughts and you change your world."
— Norman Vincent Peale

Heartbreak tests your mental and emotional strength, often leaving you feeling vulnerable, lost, and overwhelmed. But resilience isn't about avoiding pain—it's about learning how to navigate it, adapt, and emerge stronger. Building a resilient mindset helps you face future challenges with confidence and stability. This chapter explores practical ways to develop emotional resilience and cultivate a stronger mindset.

Understanding Emotional Resilience

Emotional resilience is your ability to recover from setbacks, adapt to change, and continue moving forward despite adversity. It doesn't mean you won't feel pain-*it simply means you'll have the tools to manage it without being consumed by it.*

Strength In Adversity

Ananya, a young entrepreneur from Chennai, faced immense emotional distress after her long-term relationship ended unexpectedly. The heartbreak affected her business focus, leading to financial struggles. Instead of letting it define her, she adopted a growth mindset—she started therapy, practiced gratitude, and sought support from mentors. Over time, she rebuilt both her emotional strength and her business, proving that resilience is about bouncing back, not avoiding challenges.

Accept that pain is part of life but does not define you. Cultivate a mindset that sees challenges as opportunities for growth.

Developing A Growth Mindset

A growth mindset is the belief that abilities and intelligence can develop through dedication and hard work. This mindset is crucial when overcoming heartbreak because it helps you see the experience as a lesson rather than a failure.

Heartbreak can be one of the most painful and transformative experiences in life. While it often brings emotional turmoil, it also presents an opportunity for growth, self-discovery, and resilience. A growth mindset in heartbreak means viewing the pain not as a permanent wound but as a stepping stone toward healing and personal evolution. By shifting your perspective, you can turn heartbreak into a powerful catalyst for self- improvement and future happiness.

Adopting a growth mindset during heartbreak can help in several ways:

1. **Emotional Resilience** – Understanding that pain is temporary allows you to endure and overcome it.
2. **Self-Discovery** – Heartbreak often forces introspection, helping you learn more about your needs, values, and goals.
3. **Stronger Future Relationships** – Lessons learned from past experiences enable healthier connections moving forward.
4. **Increased Self-Morth** – Realizing that your value is not dependent on someone else's love builds confidence and independence.

5. **Ability to Embrace Change** – Instead of fearing uncertainty, you become more adaptable and open to new possibilities.

Recognizing the difference between these mindsets can shift how you process your emotions:

Fixed Mindset: Believes heartbreak is a sign of failure, assumes love will always end in pain, feels stuck in emotional suffering, and resists change.

Growth Mindset: Accepts heartbreak as part of life, sees pain as a teacher, believes in personal growth, and is open to new beginnings.

Develop a Growth Mindset During Heartbreak

- **Accept the Pain as Part of the Process :** Instead of resisting emotions, allow yourself to feel and process them. Healing begins with acceptance.
- **Reframe the Experience as a Learning Opportunity** Ask yourself: What did this relationship teach me about love, myself, and my needs?
- **Challenge Negative Self-Talk :** Instead of saying, "I'll never find love again," remind yourself, "This is a chapter, not the whole book of my life."
- **Focus on Personal Growth :** Use this time to invest in yourself—pursue new skills, hobbies, and passions that bring fulfillment.
- **Surround Yourself with Supportive People :** Lean on friends, family, or support groups who encourage your healing and growth.
- **Embrace the Concept of 'Yet' :** If you feel stuck, remind yourself: "I haven't healed yet, but I am on my way."
- **Practice Self-Compassion :** Be gentle with yourself. Healing is not linear, and setbacks are part of the journey.

Heartbreak can feel overwhelming, but with a growth mindset, it becomes a stepping stone to a stronger, wiser, and more fulfilled version of yourself.

By embracing the lessons, challenging limiting beliefs, and investing in personal growth, you transform pain into power. Healing takes time, but remember—you are not broken; you are evolving.

Perspective Shift

Raj, a marketing executive from Pune, initially saw his breakup as a personal failure. He believed he wasn't "good enough." However, after reading about the growth mindset, he started reframing his thoughts— seeing the breakup as an opportunity to improve himself. He took up new skills, expanded his social circle, and focused on his career. Over time, his self-perception transformed, and he found happiness independently.

Challenge negative thoughts and replace them with empowering beliefs. See failures as steppingstones to growth rather than as final judgments of your worth.

Building Emotional Regulation Skills

Resilience isn't just about pushing through pain—it's about managing emotions in a healthy way. Learning to regulate emotions helps prevent overreactions and self-destructive behaviors.

Heartbreak is an emotional storm, but learning to regulate your feelings allows you to navigate it with strength and grace. By acknowledging emotions, developing healthy coping mechanisms, and practicing self- compassion, you transform pain into growth. Emotional regulation doesn't mean suppressing feelings—it means giving yourself the tools to process them in a way that fosters healing and resilience. In time, you'll emerge stronger, wiser, and ready for new beginnings.

Emotional Mastery

Meera, a teacher from Jaipur, had a tendency to suppress her emotions after her divorce. She bottled up her feelings until they exploded in moments of frustration. Realizing the damage, she started practicing emotional awareness—naming her emotions, allowing herself to feel them, and then choosing how to respond. This helped her navigate difficult situations with a calmer and more balanced approach.

"Acknowledge your emotions without letting them control you. Practice mindfulness, meditation, or journaling to process feelings constructively."

Developing Mental Toughness

Heartbreak can shake your confidence, emotions, and sense of self. While pain is inevitable, how you respond to it determines your growth and healing. Developing mental toughness allows you to navigate heartbreak with resilience, clarity, and strength. Instead of allowing heartbreak to define you, mental toughness empowers you to rise above it, learn from the experience, and emerge stronger than before.

Mental toughness is about staying strong in difficult times, maintaining focus, and persisting despite setbacks. It is a crucial skill when healing from heartbreak, as it allows you to navigate emotional pain without losing sight of your goals and self-worth.

Strategies To Develop Mental Toughness

- **Embrace Discomfort:** Growth happens outside your comfort zone. Accept the pain of heartbreak as part of your journey rather than resisting it.
- **Reframe Negative Thoughts:** Instead of seeing yourself as a victim, view yourself as a survivor who is gaining wisdom from the experience.
- **Set Goals:** Having clear objectives can shift your focus away from pain and towards personal growth.

- **Practice Discipline:** Mental toughness thrives on routine and self-discipline. Sticking to a schedule, exercising, and maintaining commitments build resilience.
- **Practice Gratitude and Positive Thinking :** Shift your focus from what you lost to what you still have and what you can gain.
- **Challenge Limiting Beliefs :** Replace thoughts like "I'll never love again" with "I am capable of love and happiness."
- **Commit to Moving Forward :** Set goals for your personal and professional life to maintain momentum beyond heartbreak.
- **Seek Challenges:** Facing small challenges daily strengthens your ability to deal with bigger life struggles, making you mentally tougher over time.

Path To Mental Strength

Vikram, a professional athlete from Delhi, experienced a devastating breakup right before an important tournament. Instead of letting his emotions sabotage his performance, he channeled his energy into training. He reminded himself that pain was temporary, but his dreams were worth pursuing. His mental toughness not only helped him win the championship but also taught him the power of discipline and resilience.

Solution: Strengthen your mind through discipline, goal-setting, and persistence. When faced with pain, channel your energy into constructive actions rather than self-doubt.

Journey To Self-Love

Rina, a writer from Kolkata, blamed herself entirely for her breakup. She engaged in negative self-talk, constantly criticizing herself. Through self- help books and therapy, she learned about self-compassion and started changing her inner dialogue. Instead of saying, "I'm not good enough," she started saying, "I'm growing and learning." This shift allowed her to heal and rebuild her confidence.

Solution: Be kind to yourself. Replace self-judgment with self-acceptance. Engage in activities that nurture your soul, whether it's reading, art, or meditation.

Self-compassion is treating yourself with the same kindness you would offer a friend. It's about recognizing that everyone makes mistakes and deserves forgiveness.

Developing A Self-Care Routine For Mental And Physical Well-Being

Self-care is a fundamental pillar of emotional resilience. Taking care of your mind and body ensures that you have the strength to process pain and move forward. A well-structured self-care routine provides stability and a sense of control over your well-being.

Healing Through Self-Care

Sanya, a graphic designer from Bangalore, struggled with anxiety after her relationship ended. She often neglected her health, skipped meals, and isolated herself. One day, a friend suggested she create a self-care schedule, and she started small—morning walks, healthy meals, and evening journaling. Within weeks, she noticed an improvement in her mood and energy levels. Taking care of herself became an act of self-respect, reinforcing her self-worth.

Solution: Develop a daily self-care routine that includes physical activity, nutritious meals, quality sleep, and relaxation techniques. Self-care is not a luxury—it's a necessity for healing and resilience.

Daily Habits To Cultivate Self-Love And Empowerment

Cultivating self-love isn't a one-time decision; it's a daily practice. Small, consistent habits can gradually shift your mindset and strengthen your sense of self-worth.

Self-love is not a luxury; it is a necessity. At the heart of every fulfilled life lies a person who has learned to appreciate, accept, and affirm themselves despite their flaws, failures, and fears. To cultivate self-love is to recognize your own worth—not because of your achievements or how others see you, but because you are inherently valuable.

Empowerment begins with that recognition. It is born from the courage to stand up for your truth, the willingness to heal your wounds, and the decision to stop shrinking yourself to fit into boxes that were never meant for you. Many of us grow up learning to be kind to others but are rarely taught how to be kind to ourselves.

We celebrate the strengths of others, forgive their mistakes, and offer them compassion. Yet when it comes to ourselves, we become our harshest critics. The path to self-love starts by noticing this imbalance and choosing to change it. You deserve the same grace, patience, and support you offer others.

Begin by listening to the way you speak to yourself. Is your inner voice uplifting or judgmental? Replace self-criticism with compassion. Instead of saying "I'm such a failure," try "I'm learning and growing." This subtle shift in language can transform how you see yourself. Language matters. It creates your reality. Empower yourself through positive self-talk that validates your efforts and acknowledges your growth.

Self-love also means accepting your whole self—not just the parts you like or that are socially acceptable, but the messy, raw, vulnerable parts too. We all have scars, stories, and shadows. Embrace them. They make you human. They make you real.

Empowerment grows when you stop hiding your authenticity and start embracing your wholeness. You don't have to be perfect to be worthy. Your value is not tied to your productivity, your appearance, or your popularity. It lies in your existence. Start seeing yourself as someone who deserves good things, not because you've earned them, but because you are enough as you are.

Practicing self-care not just as a routine, but as a lifestyle. Feed your body with nourishment, your mind with inspiration, and your soul with love. Take time to rest, reflect, and recharge. Honor your needs without apology. When you pour into yourself, you create space to show up more fully in every area of your life.

Empowerment also comes from owning your story. Every challenge you've faced, every setback you've endured, every time you've risen after a fall— they are all part of your narrative. Don't let shame silence your journey.

Your story holds power—not just to heal you, but to inspire others. Speak your truth. Share your lessons. Step into your light even if your voice trembles. There is strength in vulnerability. The world doesn't need another masked version of perfection. It needs real people with real stories who are willing to rise despite their struggles.

"Empowerment means standing tall in your truth, knowing that your journey is valid and your voice matters. "

Daily Rituals For Self-Empowerment

Amit, a finance professional from Mumbai, found himself stuck in negative self-perception after his breakup. He constantly compared himself to others, feeling inadequate. A mentor advised him to adopt daily habits that reinforced self-love. He started each morning with affirmations, listed three things he appreciated about himself, and set small goals that made him feel accomplished. Over time, his confidence and self-esteem improved.

Solution: Incorporate habits like positive affirmations, gratitude journaling, goal-setting, and self-reflection into your daily routine. Small acts of self- love accumulate, leading to a profound transformation in how you perceive yourself.

Building emotional resilience is a journey, not an overnight transformation. It requires commitment, self-reflection, and a willingness to grow.

CHAPTER SEVEN

STEP 6 : BUILDING HEALTHIER RELATIONSHIPS IN FUTURE

"We repeat what we don't repair."

- Anonymous

Healing from heartbreak isn't just about moving on—it's also about preparing yourself for healthier, more fulfilling relationships in the future. Once you've taken the time to

rediscover yourself, the next step is understanding what makes a relationship healthy, recognizing warning signs, and building trust again. This chapter will guide you through key aspects of forming meaningful connections with others while ensuring your emotional well-being.

Understanding Healthy vs. Toxic Relationships

A healthy relationship is built on mutual respect, trust, and emotional support, while a toxic relationship often involves control, manipulation, and emotional harm. Understanding the difference between the two helps in making better relationship choices in the future.

Healthy Relationship Characteristics

- Mutual respect and support
- Open and honest communication
- Trust and reliability
- Encouragement of personal growth and individuality
- Equality in decision-making

Toxic Relationship Characteristics

- Manipulation and control
- Gaslighting and emotional abuse
- Lack of trust and constant suspicion
- Constant criticism and belittling
- Extreme jealousy or possessiveness

Path To A Healthy Relationship

Building a healthy relationship requires self-awareness, emotional intelligence, and mutual respect. Whether you are entering a new relationship or strengthening an existing one, understanding the key components of a successful partnership can help create a fulfilling and lasting bond. Healthy relationships are built on trust, communication, and shared values, allowing both partners to grow individually and together.

Open and Honest Communication

Transparent communication is substantial for any strong relationship. It involves active listening, freedom of expression, thoughts & feelings clearly, and being open to feedback. Healthy communication includes:

- Speaking honestly and respectfully • Listening without judgment
- Addressing conflicts constructively

Exercising thoughtful communication can prevent disagreements and increase emotional intimacy.

Mutual Respect and Trust

Trust is the cornerstone of a strong relationship. It is built over time through consistent actions, honesty, and reliability. Respecting each other's boundaries, opinions, and individuality fosters a sense of security and appreciation. To nurture trust and respect:

- Be honest and transparent
- Keep promises and commitments
- Support each other's personal growth

Emotional and Physical Intimacy

Emotional intimacy involves sharing feelings, thoughts, and experiences in a safe and supportive environment. Physical intimacy, whether through affection, touch, or closeness, also plays a vital role in maintaining a connection. Building intimacy includes:

- Spending quality time together
- Expressing appreciation and affection
- Being present and attentive to each other's needs

Setting Healthy Boundaries

Boundaries are essential in maintaining a balanced relationship. They help define personal space, needs, and expectations while ensuring mutual respect. Establishing healthy boundaries involves:

- Communicating personal needs and limits • Respecting each other's independence
- Balancing time together and apart

Boundaries create a sense of autonomy while reinforcing trust and connection.

Conflict Resolution and Growth

Disagreements are a natural part of any relationship. Handling conflicts in a constructive way helps strengthen the bond rather than weaken it. Healthy conflict resolution includes:

- Addressing issues calmly and respectfully
- Focusing on solutions rather than blame
- Learning from disagreements to improve the relationship

A growth mindset allows both partners to evolve and support each other's personal development.

Shared Values and Goals

Aligning on core values and long-term goals strengthens the foundation of a relationship. While differences can be enriching, having shared priorities and a vision for the future fosters harmony. Discussing important aspects such as family, career, and lifestyle helps build a unified path forward.

A healthy relationship requires effort, understanding, and continuous growth. By fostering open communication, trust, intimacy, and mutual respect, you create a partnership that is fulfilling and resilient. Embracing challenges as opportunities for growth and aligning on shared values will lead to a deeper, more meaningful connection. True love flourishes when both partners feel valued, supported, and empowered to be their best selves.

Ayesha, an architect from Hyderabad, once found herself in a relationship where she was constantly criticized and made to feel small. After ending it, she worked on building her self-worth. When she met someone new, she recognized the importance of mutual respect and open communication, ensuring she did not fall into the same toxic patterns.

Solution: Learn to identify and embrace healthy relationships by setting clear boundaries and valuing yourself enough to walk away from toxicity.

Red Flags And Green Flags To Look For

Recognizing red flags early on can prevent emotional distress, while green flags indicate a strong foundation for a lasting relationship.

Red Flags (Warning Signs):

- Love bombing (excessive attention in the beginning, followed by emotional withdrawal)
- Disrespect for your boundaries
- Frequent lying or dishonesty

- Controlling behavior disguised as concern
- A lack of accountability for their actions

Green Flags (Positive Signs):

- Respect for your personal space and individuality
- Open and consistent communication
- Ability to handle disagreements maturely
- Encouragement of your goals and aspirations
- Emotional security and trust

Realization

Rohan, a software developer from Pune, had a history of ignoring red flags in relationships. His last relationship was filled with jealousy and control, but he mistook it for love. After attending therapy, he learned to recognize unhealthy behaviors and eventually entered a balanced, respectful relationship.

Solution: Pay attention to behavioral patterns rather than just words. Trust your instincts when something feels off.

Learning To Trust Again

After experiencing heartbreak, trusting again can be difficult. Trust is the foundation of any strong relationship, but once broken, rebuilding it can feel overwhelming. Whether trust was damaged by betrayal, past experiences, or personal insecurities, learning to trust again is essential for emotional well-being and future relationships. While it takes time, patience, and self-awareness, regaining trust is possible through intentional actions and a commitment to healing.

However, carrying past pain into new relationships can prevent true emotional connection. So, we should start the process of rebuilding trust by :

Acknowledge and Process Your Feelings

Before you can rebuild trust, it's important to acknowledge your emotions. Betrayal, disappointment, and fear are natural responses to broken trust.

Suppressing these feelings can lead to resentment, so take time to process them through journaling, talking with a trusted friend, or seeking professional guidance. Recognizing your emotions is the first step toward healing.

Understand the Root Cause of Distrust

Ask yourself why you struggle with trust. Is it due to past betrayals, childhood experiences, or personal insecurities? Understanding the root cause can help you work through these issues and prevent them from affecting future relationships. Self-reflection allows you to differentiate between justified concerns and unfounded fears.

Set Healthy Boundaries

Trust is not about blind faith; it requires clear boundaries. Establishing what is acceptable and what is not helps create a safe emotional environment. Healthy boundaries include:

- Communicating expectations openly
- Expressing your needs without fear
- Recognizing red flags and respecting your own limits

By setting boundaries, you create a foundation for mutual respect and trust.

Take Small Steps

Rebuilding trust doesn't happen overnight. Start by taking small, manageable steps toward trusting again. This may include:

- Giving people the benefit of the doubt
- Allowing yourself to be vulnerable in safe situations
- Observing consistent actions over time

Patience is key. Trust grows when people prove through actions—not just words—that they are reliable and sincere.

Communicate Openly & Honestly

If your trust was broken in a relationship, open communication is crucial. Express your concerns and fears without blame, and listen to the other person's perspective. Transparent conversations can prevent misunderstandings and help both individuals work toward rebuilding trust together.

Cultivate Self-Trust

Before trusting others, it's important to trust yourself. This means:

- Listening to your intuition
- Making decisions that align with your values
- Believing in your ability to handle challenges

When you have confidence in your own judgment, trusting others becomes easier.

Embrace Forgiveness and Let Go of the Past

Forgiveness doesn't mean forgetting or excusing harmful behavior—it means freeing yourself from the burden of pain. Holding onto resentment prevents healing and makes it harder to trust again. Letting go of past wounds allows you to move forward with an open heart.

Surround Yourself with Trustworthy People

Build relationships with those who consistently demonstrate honesty, reliability, and integrity. Being around people who respect your feelings and values reinforces that trust is possible and worthwhile.

Starting to trust again is a slow & steady process that requires mindfulness, tolerance, and nerve. By acknowledging your emotions, setting boundaries, and surrounding yourself with supportive people, you can rebuild trust in a way that empowers you. Whether in friendships, romantic relationships, or professional settings, trust is a gift that strengthens connections and fosters emotional security. Through self-growth and intentional choices, you can create relationships that are built on a strong, trusting foundation.

Journey To Trust

Aniket, an entrepreneur from Bangalore, was deeply hurt when his ex- partner cheated on him. For years, he found it difficult to trust again. With the help of counseling and self-work, he slowly learned to separate past betrayal from new experiences, eventually allowing himself to love again without fear.

"Trust is rebuilt through patience and self-awareness. Avoid making assumptions based on past pain, and give new people the opportunity to prove themselves."

Communicating Effectively In New Relationships

Communication is the foundation of a strong relationship. Learning to express yourself clearly and listen to your partner prevents misunderstandings and deepens emotional bonds.

Key Aspects of Healthy Communication:

- **Active Listening:** Pay attention to understand, not just to respond.
- **Expressing Feelings Honestly:** Share emotions without fear of judgment.
- **Setting Boundaries:** Communicate what is acceptable and what isn't.
- **Handling Conflict Constructively:** Address disagreements calmly rather than letting resentment build up.
- **Checking in Regularly:** Have open conversations about how both partners feel in the relationship.

Communication Breakthrough

Simran and Kunal, a couple from Delhi, struggled with constant misunderstandings early in their relationship. They often assumed what the other was thinking rather than discussing their feelings openly. After attending a relationship workshop, they learned how to communicate openly and actively listen to each other's needs, leading to a much stronger bond.

"Practice healthy communication skills early on. Open dialogue fosters deeper connection and prevents unnecessary conflict."

Building healthier relationships after heartbreak is a journey of self- awareness, learning, and growth. By understanding what makes a relationship healthy, recognizing red and green flags, rebuilding trust, and developing strong communication skills, you prepare yourself for meaningful and fulfilling connections.

Love after heartbreak is possible—it just requires a stronger, wiser version of yourself to embrace it.

CHAPTER EIGHT

STEP 7 : MOVING FORWARD WITH PURPOSE

"Your life does not get better by chance, it gets better by change — and change begins when you move with intention."
— *Jim Rohn*

After experiencing heartbreak, it's easy to feel lost or uncertain about what comes next. However, this chapter is about reclaiming control over your life, setting meaningful goals, and

using your pain as a catalyst for growth. Whether you choose to embrace singlehood, pursue new passions, or prepare yourself for love again, moving forward with purpose ensures that your future is shaped by intention rather than circumstance.

In the fast-paced world we live in, many people find themselves drifting through life without a clear direction. Days blur into weeks, and weeks into years, leaving behind a trail of unfulfilled dreams and unanswered questions. At the root of this restlessness often lies one central void: a lack of purpose. Purpose is not just a lofty idea or spiritual concept—it is the internal compass that gives meaning to our actions, guides our decisions, and fuels our resilience during tough times.

What Is Purpose?

Purpose is the reason behind our existence. It is the deeper motivation that drives us beyond routine survival—beyond eating, working, or sleeping. Purpose ties our everyday actions to a larger meaning, giving us a sense of identity, direction, and belonging. It is not necessarily tied to a job or role; rather, it can be expressed through relationships, creativity, service, learning, or any endeavor that resonates with our inner values.

Why Purpose Matters

1. Clarity in Chaos

Life is full of uncertainties—career changes, health issues, heartbreaks, and losses. Without purpose, these moments can feel like random blows. But a strong sense of purpose offers perspective. It helps you ask, "What can I learn from this?" or "How can this experience shape me toward who I want to become?"

2. Motivation and Drive

When you wake up knowing that your day serves a bigger goal, even the mundane tasks take on new meaning. Purpose is a powerful motivator. Athletes like Serena Williams don't wake up at 5 AM every day just for medals. They are driven by a purpose—to be the best, to inspire others, to push the limits of human potential.

In everyday life, think of a mother working two jobs to give her children a better future. Her purpose—to provide and protect—is what sustains her. Without purpose, such struggle could easily lead to burnout. With it, even the hardest days feel worthwhile.

3. Resilience During Hardship

Purpose does not shield us from pain, but it makes pain more bearable. People with a strong sense of purpose recover faster from trauma, cope better with stress, and show higher levels of emotional stability.

Consider Malala Yousafzai. After surviving a gunshot wound from the Taliban for advocating girls' education, she didn't retreat into fear. Instead, her purpose strengthened. She went on to become the youngest Nobel Peace Prize laureate, continuing to fight for education globally. Her suffering became part of her mission.

4. Fulfillment and Happiness

True fulfillment doesn't come from wealth or fame—it comes from living in alignment with your values and making a meaningful impact. Studies show that people with a sense of purpose live longer, report higher life satisfaction, and are less prone to depression.

Tony Robbins often says, "Success without fulfillment is the ultimate failure." Purpose transforms success into something deeply satisfying. You're not just ticking off achievements; you're living a story that feels significant.

Purpose in Innovation

Steve Jobs wasn't just building gadgets; he believed in "putting a dent in the universe." His purpose was to blend technology with art and simplify lives through innovation. Even after being ousted from Apple, he returned years later not for money, but because he believed in what he was building. His purpose was so strong, it reshaped entire industries.

Purpose Through Empowerment

Born into poverty and surviving years of trauma, Oprah could have given up many times. But her purpose—to use her voice to uplift others—became her guiding light. Her show wasn't just entertainment; it was a platform for healing, growth, and social change. Today, her influence continues through schools, foundations, and media channels dedicated to personal empowerment.

Purpose in Education

Anand Kumar, a mathematician from India, started the "Super 30" program to train underprivileged students for the IIT entrance exam. Despite his own struggles with poverty, he found purpose in educating others. His dedication transformed countless lives, turning students from slums into engineers, scientists, and professionals. His story shows that purpose doesn't require wealth—only will.

Finding Your Purpose

Not everyone wakes up knowing their life's mission. And that's okay. Purpose is something you discover, not declare. Here are a few ways to start the journey:

- **Reflect on Your Passions and Pains:** What makes you come alive? What injustice makes your blood boil? Often, purpose is hidden in both your joy and your wounds.
- **Ask, "Whom Do I Want to Help?"** Purpose is often outward-facing. It's about how your gifts can serve others.
- **Follow Curiosity:** Don't wait for lightning. Explore. Read. Travel. Talk to people. Pay attention to what energizes you.
- **Embrace Change:** Your purpose can evolve. A student may find purpose in learning; later, in teaching. A parent's purpose may shift once children grow. That's normal.
- **Stay Patient:** Purpose grows through experience. Don't rush the process. As the saying goes, "Clarity comes from engagement, not thought."

Purpose is not a luxury reserved for the spiritually elite or the ultra-successful. It is a necessity for every human soul. Without it, life becomes routine and reactive. With it, every moment becomes intentional and inspired. Purpose gives you a reason to get up when life knocks you down. It turns pain into power and routine into ritual.

Whether you're 18 or 80, it's never too early—or too late—to discover your why. You don't have to change the world overnight. Start small. But start today. Because a life with purpose is not just a life well-lived; it's a life that leaves a legacy.

Setting Goals For Your Personal And Emotional Growth

Healing is not just about letting go of the past but about consciously shaping your future. **Setting goals*aligned to your purpose*** helps you move forward with clarity and direction.

Significance of Goal-Setting :

- Provides a sense of purpose
- Keeps you motivated and focused
- Encourages self-improvement and personal growth
- Helps track progress and celebrate achievements

Types Of Goals To Set:

1. **Emotional Goals:** Work on self-love, self-acceptance, and emotional resilience.
2. **Career and Educational Goals:** Upskill yourself, pursue higher education, or advance in your profession.
3. **Physical and Mental Well-being Goals:** Establish a self- care routine that includes fitness, meditation, or therapy.
4. **Social and Relationship Goals:** Reconnect with old friends, set healthy relationship standards, and expand your social circle.

Pain, though deeply challenging, has the potential to transform into a source of strength and purpose. When we experience heartbreak, loss, or personal struggles, we can choose to let our pain define us or use it as fuel to create something meaningful. By channeling pain into acts of service, creative expression, or personal growth, we not only heal ourselves but also inspire and uplift others.

One of the most powerful ways to transform pain into purpose is by supporting others who are going through similar experiences. Whether through mentorship, volunteering, or simply offering a listening ear, sharing your journey can provide comfort and hope to those in need.

Volunteering: Engaging in community service, crisis support groups, or nonprofit work allows you to give back while finding personal fulfillment.

Mentorship: Guiding someone who is facing struggles similar to what you have endured can reinforce your own growth while offering invaluable support to them.

Sharing Your Story: Writing, speaking, or connecting with others through support groups can create a sense of solidarity and healing.

Helping others not only shifts focus away from personal suffering but also instills a sense of purpose and fulfillment that fosters resilience.

Creative Outlets: Expressing And Healing Through Art

Creativity is a robust instrument for emotional release and self-discovery. Whether through writing, music, painting, or other forms of artistic expression, creative outlets help process emotions in a constructive and healing manner.

Writing: Journaling, poetry, or storytelling allows for deep introspection and helps articulate emotions that might be difficult to express verbally.

Music and Dance: Engaging in music or dance can be a cathartic way to release pent-up emotions and find joy amid pain.

Visual Art: Painting, sculpting, or digital art can serve as a nonverbal way to channel feelings and create something beautiful from personal struggles.

Creative expression enables the transformation of pain into something tangible, allowing for reflection and personal empowerment.

Building A Life Of Purpose Beyond Pain

The journey from pain to purpose is about rediscovering who you are beyond your struggles. Taking time to set new goals, explore new passions, and cultivate gratitude can help rebuild a fulfilling life. By choosing to grow from adversity, you create a path that is not only healing for yourself but also inspiring for others.

Pain, while inevitable, does not have to be the end of the story. By using personal hardships as a catalyst for helping others and expressing emotions through creative outlets, pain can be transformed into purpose. The process of healing becomes a journey of meaning, connection, and resilience, proving that even in the darkest moments, light can emerge through acts of service and creativity.

Ways To Turn Pain Into Purpose:

Helping Others: Join support groups, volunteer, or mentor someone going through a similar situation.

Creative Outlets: Express emotions through writing, painting, music, or any form of art.

Sharing Your Story: Start a blog, a podcast, or a YouTube channel to inspire others.

Entrepreneurial Ventures: Many successful businesses stem from personal experiences—consider starting a venture that aligns with your passions.

Raghav, a software engineer from Bangalore, went through a painful divorce. Instead of drowning in sorrow, he started a mental health support community for men dealing with emotional struggles. Today, his initiative has helped hundreds find a safe space to heal.

Solution: Channel pain into something meaningful. Find an avenue that allows you to express yourself while contributing positively to the world.

Embracing Singlehood vs. Preparing for Love Again

After heartbreak, the journey forward presents two equally valuable paths: embracing singlehood as a time of self-growth and independence or preparing to open your heart to love again. Both paths require healing, self- reflection, and an understanding of personal needs and desires. Choosing between them—or even balancing both—depends on where you are in your emotional journey and what fulfills you the most.

Embracing singlehood is not about resigning to loneliness—it's about rediscovering yourself and reclaiming your identity. Often after a breakup or a period of emotional entanglement, we forget who we are outside of a relationship.

This is your time to heal, to grow, and to learn what truly makes you feel alive. Being single offers the priceless gift of self-reflection and independence. It allows you to pursue passions, deepen friendships, and make choices that are fully your own. More importantly, it gives you the space to understand your past patterns in relationships and break the cycles that no longer serve you.

Singlehood isn't a void waiting to be filled—it's a season of wholeness, a phase where you cultivate self-love so fierce that it sets the standard for how others treat you. On the other side of healing lies a different kind of readiness: the courage to love again. Preparing for love doesn't mean rushing into the next available relationship. It means approaching love with a sense of wholeness rather than lack.

When you're emotionally grounded and at peace with being alone, you're no longer searching for someone to complete you—you're seeking someone to complement the life you've already built. Preparation for love involves vulnerability, openness, and the wisdom gained from your singlehood. It'sabout recognizing red flags early, communicating your needs clearly, and honoring your boundaries.

Whether you remain single or open yourself to love again, both paths require intention, awareness, and a deep connection with yourself.

Ultimately, the goal isn't to find someone who fixes you—it's to become someone who doesn't need fixing and chooses love freely, not out of fear but from abundance.

Embracing Singlehood: Finding Strength In Independence

Singlehood is an opportunity to reconnect with yourself, explore new interests, and build a fulfilling life on your own terms. Rather than viewing it as a period of waiting, it can be a time of transformation and self- discovery.

Self-Discovery: Use this time to explore your passions, set personal goals, and understand your core values.

Building Confidence: Cultivate self-worth independent of external validation. Strengthening your sense of self will help you establish healthier relationships in the future.

Enjoying Freedom: Without the constraints of a relationship, you have the space to travel, take risks, and focus on personal ambitions without compromise.

Strengthening Other Relationships: Invest time in friendships, family, and personal development to build a strong support network.

Choosing to embrace singlehood is not about rejecting love but about ensuring that when love comes, you enter it as a whole, fulfilled person rather than seeking completion through another.

Preparing For Love Again: Opening Your Heart To New Possibilities

When the time feels right, opening yourself up to love again requires trust, emotional readiness, and a clear understanding of what you want from a relationship.

Healing Past Mounds: Ensure that unresolved pain or baggage from previous relationships does not shape new connections. Forgiveness—of yourself and others—can be a crucial step.

Defining Relationship Standards: Take the time to understand what you truly desire in a partner and what values align with yours.

Practicing Vulnerability: Being open to love means being open to vulnerability. Trust takes time to build and takes time, and allowing yourself to connect deeply is fundamental.

Mindful Dating: Approach new relationships with curiosity rather than urgency. Enjoy the process of meeting new people without rushing into something for the sake of companionship.

Striking A Balance: Honoring Your Own Pace

There is no set timeline for healing or for choosing between singlehood and love. Some may find joy in their independence for years before considering a relationship, while others may feel ready for love sooner. What matters most is listening to yourself, embracing your journey, and making choices that align with your happiness and well-being.

Whether you choose to embrace singlehood or prepare for love again, both paths offer valuable lessons and opportunities for growth. The key is to honor your personal journey, take the time to heal, and step forward with self-awareness and confidence. Love—whether for yourself or for another —should always come from a place of wholeness, not longing. No matter which path you take, fulfillment and happiness come from within.

Priya, a fashion designer from Chennai, used to define her happiness through relationships. After a tough breakup, she consciously chose to stay single for a while. She traveled, learned yoga, and reconnected with herself. Eventually, she realized she didn't need a partner to feel complete.

Preparing For Love Again:

- Ensure that you are emotionally healed before seeking a new relationship.
- Set clear relationship standards and boundaries.
- Take things slow and allow trust to build naturally.
- Choose a partner who complements your growth rather than completes you.

Aryan, a marketing executive from Pune, was hesitant to date again after his painful breakup. However, when he met someone who aligned with his values, he approached the relationship with maturity and patience. Because he took time to heal first, he was able to build a healthier, more balanced relationship.

Solution: Whether you choose to remain single or love again, ensure that your decision comes from a place of self-awareness and not fear of loneliness.

Moving forward with purpose is about reclaiming your life and shaping it into something meaningful. By setting goals, channeling pain into purpose, and making conscious decisions about love, you empower yourself to build a fulfilling future. Healing is not about forgetting the past; it's about using it as a stepping stone to a brighter, more intentional tomorrow.

CHAPTER NINE

A NEW YOU

"The old you has to die so the new you can be born."
— *Joel Osteen*

As you reach the final stage of your healing journey, it's important to take a step back and reflect on the progress you've made. The pain that once felt overwhelming has now transformed into strength. The heartbreak that seemed insurmountable has become a lesson, shaping you into a wiser, more resilient version of yourself. This chapter is dedicated to celebrating your growth, providing final words of encouragement, and offering resources for continued self-discovery.

Reflection On Progress Made

Healing from heartbreak is not a linear process; it is filled with highs and lows. However, with each passing day, you've taken small yet significant steps toward a new and empowered version of yourself. Reflecting on this progress helps solidify your growth and reinforce the changes you've made.

Signs Of Your Progress:

- You no longer feel controlled by past emotions or memories.
- You've established healthier coping mechanisms for dealing with pain.
- You have a clearer sense of self and what you want from life.

- You embrace self-love and recognize your own worth.
- You've cultivated healthier relationships and boundaries.
- You feel excited about the future rather than dwelling on the past.

Exercise: A Letter To Your Past Self

One way to acknowledge your progress is to write a letter to your past self - the version of you who was hurting at the beginning of this journey. Share what you have learned, how you have changed, and offer reassurance that everything turned out okay. This routine acts as a reminder of your progress and a indication of your strength.

"Healing is an ongoing journey, and there will always be moments when old wounds resurface. However, the difference now is that you have the tools, mindset, and resilience to handle these challenges. "

Moving forward, remember :

You Are Enough

You do not need validation from anyone else to feel whole. Your worth is inherent, and you are deserving of love, respect, and happiness—regardless of your relationship status.

Pain is Temporary, Growth is Permanent

The heartbreak you experienced does not define you. It was simply a chapter in your life, and you have emerged stronger because of it.

You Have Control Over Your Happiness

While circumstances may be out of your control, your response to them is not. Choose to focus on joy, gratitude, and self-improvement rather than dwelling on what was lost. It is not something you find; it is something you create.

At its core, happiness is an internal state. While external circumstances can certainly influence our emotions, they do not have the power to define our long-term well-being—unless we allow them to. Every day, we are given opportunities to choose how we respond to life. The power lies not in avoiding the storms, but in learning how to dance in the rain.

So breathe deeply. Pause. Listen. Remember who you are beneath the noise. The love, the peace, the joy you seek is not out there—it is within. And when you choose to tap into that inner reservoir, you become unshakable.

You become a light for yourself and for others. And most importantly, you remember the truth: you have always had the power to be happy—because you are the source of it.

"Love Will Find You When the Time is Right"

If you choose to open your heart again, trust that the right person will come at the right time. Until then, continue to focus on being the best version of yourself.

Every Ending Is A New Beginning

This is not just the end of a relationship; it is the beginning of a new chapter in your life—one that is filled with endless possibilities, self-discovery, and happiness.

Heartbreak often feels like a definitive ending—a painful closure to something once cherished. However, every ending carries within it the seed of a new beginning. While the grief of a lost relationship is real, it also presents an opportunity for growth, self-discovery, and transformation. The journey beyond heartbreak is not just about moving on but about moving forward, embracing the unknown with hope and resilience.

Welcoming New Opportunities

Heartbreak can feel like a closed door, but it often redirects you toward new possibilities. The end of one chapter allows for unexpected experiences, relationships, and opportunities to enter your life.

- **New Connections:** Surround yourself with supportive friends and remain open to meeting new people who align with your values.
- **Exploring Different Perspectives:** Travel, read, or engage in new activities that expand your worldview.
- **Embracing Change:** See change not as a loss but as a transition leading to greater things.

Rather than fearing change, view it as an open road leading to new adventures. Sometimes, heartbreak shakes us out of complacency, urging us to make choices we wouldn't have otherwise considered. Whether it's taking up a new hobby, switching careers, or simply reshaping your mindset, every new step is an opportunity to rewrite your story in a way that serves your happiness and well-being.

Choosing To See Hope In Endings

Every heartbreak is a turning point. It is a chance to rebuild stronger, wiser, and more aligned with your true self. Instead of dwelling on what was lost, shift your focus to what can be gained. The future holds endless possibilities, and the end of one love story is simply the beginning of another—perhaps the love story of self-growth, adventure, or even a new romantic journey.

Letting go doesn't mean forgetting; it means making peace with the past and allowing yourself to embrace the present. Choosing hope over despair means believing that what's ahead is just as—if not more—beautiful than what's behind. Shift your mindset to gratitude for the experiences you had rather than longing for what could have been.

Trusting That Love Will Find You Again

While healing from heartbreak, it's easy to fall into the belief that love may never return. However, love is not something that happens once; it is something we are capable of experiencing in different ways and at different times in our lives. Trust that love will find you again when you are ready.

Instead of following love, focus on becoming the best version of yourself. When you are whole and at peace, the right people will naturally be drawn to you. Love is not a destination but an ongoing journey—one that starts with self-love and extends outward.

No ending is truly final. Heartbreak, as painful as it may be, is not a dead end but a bridge to a new phase of life. When you choose to embrace change, trust the process, and step forward with courage, you'll discover that every ending is, in reality, a beautiful new beginning. The key is to shift your perspective from loss to opportunity, from sadness to renewal, and from heartbreak to personal evolution.

As one chapter closes, another begins—one where you are stronger, wiser, and ready to embrace the beauty of what lies ahead.

Resources For Continued Self-Discovery

The journey of self-discovery does not end once the heartbreak fades; it is an ongoing process that continues to shape and define you. Here are some resources to help guide your journey:

- **Courses & Morkshops:** Online platforms like Coursera, Udemy, and MasterClass offer courses on mindfulness, personal growth, and resilience.
- **Journaling & Reflection:** Writing prompts for self-discovery can help you understand your emotions, set goals, and track progress.
- **Meditation & Spiritual Practices:** Apps like Headspace and Insight Timer offer guided meditations to help with healing and clarity.
- **Therapy & Coaching:** Seeking professional support through therapy or life coaching can provide valuable tools for healing and growth.

You can also reach out to me at insta - deepalifecoach

No ending is truly final. Heartbreak, as painful as it may be, is not a dead end but a bridge to a new phase of life. When you choose to embrace change, trust the process, and step forward with courage, you'll discover that every ending is, in reality, a beautiful new beginning. The key is to shift your perspective from loss to opportunity, from sadness to renewal, and from heartbreak to personal evolution.

As one chapter closes, another begins—one where you are stronger, wiser, and ready to embrace the beauty of what lies ahead.

Journaling Prompts For Continued Growth:

1. What are three things I have learned about myself through this experience?
2. What are my biggest strengths, and how can I use them to build the life I want?
3. How do I want to feel one year from now, and what steps can I take to get there?
4. What does my ideal life look like, and what is one thing I can do today to move closer to it?

Embracing The Future With Confidence

Moving forward after heartbreak requires trust in oneself and in the future. Confidence is not about having all the answers but about believing in your ability to handle whatever comes next.

Practice **Self-Compassion** while entering into thi state of you life. Be kind to yourself during this transition. Understand that healing takes time, and setbacks are part of growth.

Visualize Your ideal future - Instead of focusing on what was lost, imagine what you want to create in your life. Set intentions and take steps toward your goals.

Step Out of Your Comfort Zone - Growth happens when you challenge yourself. Whether it's trying a new activity, meeting new people, or traveling solo, every new experience builds confidence.

Surround Yourself with Positivity - Engage with people who uplift you and environments that encourage growth.

Confidence grows when you prove to yourself that you can navigate change. Each small achievement, from rediscovering joy in hobbies to setting and reaching new goals, adds to your sense of empowerment. Instead of fearing the future, embrace it with excitement and openness.

You have come a long way, and the best part is that your journey is just initiating. You now have the wisdom, strength, and resilience to build a life filled with purpose, passion, and joy. Whether you choose to embrace singlehood, explore new opportunities, or open your heart to love again, the most important thing is that you do so from a place of self-awareness and confidence.

"You are not broken. You are not lost. You are simply in the process of becoming the person you were always meant to be. "

This is your time to shine. Keep moving forward, keep growing, and most importantly—never stop believing in yourself.

*"**The best is yet to come.**"*

About The Author

Deepa is a relationship coach, writer, and spiritual seeker who has guided individuals through the tender landscapes of heartbreak, healing, and self-discovery for several years. Her work is rooted in compassion, clarity, and the belief that true transformation begins when we learn to sit with our pain and listen to our own hearts.

While her heart lives in the world of healing and connection, Deepa also brings with her over 17 years of experience in the IT industry as a coder and solution architect. This unique blend of structure and soul adds depth to her approach, allowing her to guide others with both grounded wisdom and intuitive sensitivity.

When she's not writing or coaching, Deepa finds peace in the cooking, joy in spiritual exploration, and purpose in helping others reconnect with their true selves. Her voice is that of a trusted friend—calm, kind, and encouraging—reminding you that healing is possible, and happiness is already yours to claim.